MW01591666

Basketball: King of Indiana

by

Gary Lee Smith

authorHOUSE™

1663 LIBERTY DRIVE, SUITE 200
BLOOMINGTON, INDIANA 47403
(800) 839-8640
WWW.AUTHORHOUSE.COM

First published by AuthorHouse 07/18/05

ISBN: 1-4208-5285-X (sc)
ISBN: 1-4208-5284-1 (dj)

Library of Congress Control Number: 2005904694

Printed in the United States of America
Bloomington, Indiana

This book is printed on acid-free paper.

This book is dedicated to my parents.

Some people think of the "good old days" and some think of the "bad old days". I'm thinking the "old days" good or bad with this book. It is true, they don't make things the way they used to, they don't do things the way they used to and the times are not what they used to be. What if time could be made to stand still? This possibility has been explored well by a short book by Natalie Babbitt that was turned into a full-length movie by Walt Disney Pictures' named *Tuck Everlasting.* Never means never. It is natural that time moves on. Each Christmas my family traditionally sits down and watches the video movie *The Christmas Story.* *The Christmas Story* is a good reminder of my early days in Indiana. With many doubts, like who is going to read it, I am encouraged by thinking, "you can do it" and "you got it." My English teachers may rise up shouting "No, oh-no." However, after going to the bookstore and looking around at the books, books and more books, I cannot help but be further encouraged. Who does read all those books? The part of time I can directly write about will soon be losing those of us who lived it. This was a period when prosperity returned after depression and war. It was a time when new, reliable, fast, powerful cars became the things to have and better roads began to greatly expand the territory. New schools were needed and small school consolidation was on the horizon. Television brought visual images of events only imagined before and the world's events and entertainment came to us and appeared in black and white right in our living rooms. And a great debate was raging in Indiana as to whether a small high school could win the greatest prize of all – the Indiana State Basketball Championship. You may have seen the movie *Hoosiers* telling the story of a small town basketball team winning the Indiana State Basketball Championship. You may have thought the story was exaggerated. It is a great movie and it has some great lines in it. However, the real life story of a small school, small town, Milan High School winning the Indiana State Basketball Championship shows the movie to be far from exaggerated. The "Milan Miracle" is the greatest sports story I know. Its impact on the human spirit cannot be exaggerated and to those of us who witnessed the times and games, the miracle has lived --and lives --on. Basketball was King of Indiana.

I was able to refer to the sports story clippings I had put into a scrapbook from *The Daily Clintonian*, *Terre Haute Tribune* and *The Indianapolis Star*. *The Daily Clintonian* microfilm was referred to in the Clinton Indiana Public Library. Also useful for more detailed information is the "History of Indiana High School Basketball" called *Hoosier Hysteria, Ninth and Final Edition --1997*, written by Herb Schwomeyer. *The Greatest Basketball Story Ever Told* written by Greg Guffey contains not only the detailed story of the Milan Indians high school basketball, but gives updates and interview comments by the players and coach through 1993. These books are available on the Internet from the Indiana Basketball Hall of Fame. In the Clinton Indiana Public Library is a researched history of Clinton Indiana titled *Clinton on the Wabash* by Louise Booth. The Methodist Church is a historical site. The Clinton high school gymnasium has been restored for those who would care to visit. The Bridgeton gristmill is operational and being restored. The release of the DVD version of *Hoosiers* has the black and white television coverage of the 1954 Indiana State Basketball Championship game between Milan and Muncie Central.

Recently I attended the 50th Clinton High School Graduation Reunion for the class of 1954 and was impressed by the unusually close relationships that still exist. Many of my high school classmates met regularly and know where all classmates are located.

Thank you to Diane Ristow who took the time to edit my often-

loose interpretation of the English language and grammar rules.

Table of Contents

In The Beginning

It is said by some that a child learns 50% of his knowledge by age six. A young child learns 80% of all he will ever know by the age of eight years. A child's value system is set by the age of 12 years. These were my Indiana years. This was Basketball Country.

I was born in Kokomo, Indiana in August 1936. It was not easy, my mother said. The summer of 1936 was one of the hottest ever on record and air conditioning was a luxury not available. My earliest memory is of my father looking at and bringing home a 1936 Ford car sometime in 1938. When I was three years old, we moved to Indianapolis (where my younger brother was born, which I don't re-member anything about). I only recall being taken to the ice cream store and seeing fire engines while living in Indianapolis. We lived close to some railroad yards and in the summer fire engines would race down our street. When I asked what for, someone gave me the explanation it was to make the fire engines "redder". It was a relative who used to take me to get the ice cream at a nearby store, probably in those days a corner drug store. Our family moved from Indianapolis to Clinton when I was age five. It was a somewhat strange set of events that now resulted in my father returning to Clinton. Dad had graduated from Clinton High School in 1928, having moved there from Bridgeton in 1927. My Grandfather and Grandmother made the move to nearby Clinton seeking work and Grandfather obtained a blacksmith job working in the coal mines. My Grandparents left Clinton after a short stay when the Klu Klux Klan (KKK) became aggressive in the coalmines and Grandfather refused to join them.

Clinton, with a population then of about 7,000, is a small, western Indiana town on the banks of the Wabash River in southern Vermillion County. Vermillion County borders eastern Illinois and is located north from Vigo County, which contains the much larger and better-known town of Terre Haute. Newport, a smaller town near the center of Vermillion County, is the county seat with the courthouse. Cayuga in the northern part of the county is the location of the County Fair Grounds. Clinton was a Sectional and Regional town for the Indiana State High School Basketball Tournament. Sectional tournament games were played in 64 locations, covering the whole state of Indiana, to narrow the total state tournament field to 64 teams. Sectional winners then went on to one of the 16 Regionals held on the following weekend to further narrow the tournament field to 16 teams. Regional winners then proceeded on to one of the four Semifinals held a week later to narrow the field to four teams. Finals were played in the Butler Fieldhouse in Indianapolis a week later to determine the Indiana State Tournament Champion. After the Sectionals, two tournament games were played on Saturday afternoon at each site to determine the teams to play later in the Saturday night game. All team pairings were drawn before the tournament started. Over 700 high school teams played for the State Championship of Indiana. The Clinton Sectional winner moved on to a Regional site that rotated each year between Clinton, Attica, Crawfordsville and Greencastle. The Regional winner then went on to Indianapolis where the Semifinals were played in the Butler University Fieldhouse. It was an early introduction application of math, geography and basketball excitement.

The Sectional was played at Clinton because it had the largest gym. The Sectional tournament was composed of 16 teams from Vermillion County and Parke County. Parke County is directly to the east and connected to Vermillion County by bridges over the Wabash River at Clinton and Montezuma. Rockville was the largest town in Parke County and the county seat. Clinton was the largest town in the Sectional and had the largest high school enrollment. Clinton High School had about 400 students in Grades 9-12. This translated to about 200 eligible boys for the sports programs. There were no equivalent girls sports programs. The Clinton gym was built in 1936 with a seating capacity of 2,100. It was made possible by Federal Emergency Administration of Public Works Project No. Ind. 1076R. The plaque in the gymnasium entrance reads "Practical Arts Building – This Building Dedicated to the Youth of Our City." Beneath the gym were the Home Economics, Shop and Band classrooms. The gym was a well-built brick structure with concrete ramps and wood bench seats. Typical of high school gyms in the area, the gym had a stage at one-basket end and entrance doors at the other. There was a built-in imposing wood scorer's desk in the middle of on the "Home Team" side of the basketball court. The highly varnished basketball court floor was do not step on with shoes, hollowed space. Large windows with many small, opaque, chicken wire reinforced windowpanes were located on each court-side of the gym above the last row of the bleachers. These large windows had smaller swing out window sections that were opened to let in air when the gym became too warm. The seats curved around to the entrance with a small balcony area at the end over the entrance. During regular home basketball games the band sat in one of the end sections on the home team side. The competing teams' players sat on opposite the side of the front edge of the stage. The electric scoreboard (with loud horn) was mounted to the right of the stage, high on the wall, on the same side as the "Home Team."

The gym was located on one corner of the school block. On the other corners were the Central Grade School (Grades 1-6), Clinton Junior High School (Grades 7-8) and the Clinton Senior High School (Grades 9-12). The grade school was a smaller, two story, and red brick building that was surrounded on three sides by a playground.

There was a tall flagpole out front. Right next to the gym was a super dirt area that we used for marbles. The two-story Clinton Volunteer Fire Department Station and school power plant were located between the Junior and Senior High Schools together with a large, towering, brick smokestack. The Clinton School Superintendent's and School Nurse's offices were in a small wooden, house-like building located between the High School and the gym. The junior and senior high schools had separate principals, but were really operated as one school with grades 7-12. The homerooms for grades 7-8 were in the building called Junior High School. Classes could be in either building. The school library was in the Junior High. The Senior High building had a large "study hall" consisting of long rows (around 12 as I recall) of desks (about 24 to each row as I recall). The study hall was also the homeroom for the sophomore, junior and senior classes. The seniors sat nearest the windows. There was a no parking zone all around the entire school block, except when school was out. Most special events included both junior and senior high schools. For example, any basketball or football pep rally or sports awards events meant that all students grades 7-12 were gathered into the gym. Events sometimes even included the Central Grade School students.

6

Clinton School Block

The Clinton Main Street business district was three blocks long and the school block was on Third Street one block over from the middle block. Clinton also had a small business district of scattered businesses on Ninth Street and that area was called "Little Italy." Many residents of Clinton were of Italian background. Clinton had a large Catholic Church and Sacred Heart was the Catholic grade school for grades 1-8. The Catholic school was the envy of the other grade schools because it had a much more robust sports program. The Catholic Church also had large church bells and the sound of their ringing was a part of the environment of the southern

7

part of Clinton. There were numerous small neighborhood taverns and grocery stores spread throughout the town. The C&EI (Chicago and Eastern Illinois) railroad intersected Main Street at the north end of the business district before crossing Water Street, the first street in town running along the Wabash River. A single-track railroad bridge crossed the Wabash River. The condition of the railroad bridge was such that trains slowed to a crawl while crossing. Just before crossing the bridge, next to the railroad tracks on Water Street, were the Indiana Public Service Company Substation and Maintenance Offices where my dad worked.

Wabash River

Our new Clinton home had a large concrete and brick front porch, living room, dining room, kitchen, two bedrooms, a den, small back porch, large basement and detached single garage behind the house. The front porch was great to store our tricycles, pedal station wagon and scooter. The porch had several concrete steps leading down to the sidewalk that my brother and I could noisily bounce our tricycle, pedal car and scooter vehicles down, proclaiming to the neighborhood it was playtime. We had good cement highways (sidewalks) to the corners of the block (as far as we were supposed to go). The concrete sidewalk pretend roadways were courtesy of the nationwide PWA (Public Works Administration). They were but one of the many PWA projects completed in Clinton during the De-pression. A neighbor also had a narrow sidewalk extending along the side of their house. This sidewalk pretend road gave us kids the feel of the narrow roads common in those days.

Out the back door was a small wood porch with several steps down to the backyard. The area under the back porch became one of my favorite play areas thanks to the plentiful dirt. Naturally we also had a sandbox, but it was smaller and sand made it difficult to create water floods with the hose. Down the alley was a little

9

grocery store. I would be sent down to the store often to pickup a loaf of bread for 10 cents. Once in awhile I would get to buy one of those little fruit pies to eat or have an orange Popsicle. We learned to watch for the ice truck to stop at the store or in the neighborhood. Then we would pester and beg for the driver to provide some of those great chips of ice to eat. For a short while, a girl lived down the alley and I was invited to one of the very few parties I can re-member. It was a birthday party and cutout paper dolls were the "in" gift for girls. Down the alley was a vacant field full of tall weeds. This vacant field was a good site for our numerous war games. The enemy flag was a sunflower sticking out high over the weeds and it became the object of our grimy, dirt ball, dust explosion grenades. When we weren't shooting the wartime enemies of the United States and mankind, we were running up and down the alley, in and out of garages, gunning down the criminal elements of society using our Gangbuster's Tommy Guns.

I don't think there was a formal kindergarten school available. I vaguely remember going to something and taking my cheap toy drum with wooden drum sticks. I don't recall being asked back.

Grades 1-3

Our house was on Third Street, three plus blocks south from Central Grade School. Just after reaching the age of five, I entered Central Grade School in September 1941. Central Grade School had the first three grades on the first floor and grades 4-6 were up the wide wooden stairs on the second floor. I walked to school; there was no bus service for the town folks (and Central Grade School was all town folks). It was drilled into our heads to watch out for cars. There were Sixth Grade Patrol Boys on the school block corner. My walk to school also crossed one of the busiest streets in town – Elm Street – and it was necessary to be careful. It was, however, enough of a walk to get into other sorts of trouble. I got into big trouble for hiding in the large drive through lumber storage shed of the lumberyard that I was supposed to walk past. I was caught inside the piles of lumber with my "girl friend" listening to the people go by on the sidewalk outside the storage shed. It must have been fun while it lasted.

The World Wars brought some good news to the depressed economic area. The Wabash Ordnance Plant was to be built by the Federal Government between Clinton and Newport. Two thousand construction workers would be needed; 3,200 permanent jobs would be created. E.I. DuPont was given the contract and an employment office opened in Clinton. Soon housing became in short supply with building at a standstill because of the war. Homes with extra rooms were turned into rooming houses. Work trains left Clinton daily for the new plant. Women began applying for jobs and joining the wartime workforce.

My first inside-the-Clinton-High-School-gym memory was an early grade school participation in a "Victory" program of some sort. I was selected to play "Buster Brown" and carry a garden hoe. This program was probably related to the individual, home grown gardens, nicknamed "Victory Gardens" that were encouraged during

World War II. My role was to march in with others and to be a part of a court sized "V" spelled out on the basketball floor and pretend to "hoe." I thought that the Buster Brown getup was ridiculous and at that early age had some opinions. I don't remember where that costume came from or what became of it. I don't recall how much of a battle I put up, but what mom said always went!

Restored Clinton High School Gym

The World Wars were ever-present realities. The 1943 Clinton High School Annual dedicated the yearbook as follows:

"A Boy Went Forth ------"

To those boys of Clinton High School from the Class of 1943, who have gone or who are to go forth to the service of their country, we, the Class of 1943, in humble and most sincere appreciation, do dedicate this issue of Old Gold and Black.

To preserve a dream, "an American Dream, that dream of a land in which life should be better and richer and fuller for every man, with opportunity for each according to his ability or achievement," you have gone. To you, our youth, we pay tribute.

To my parents, education was always serious business. For example, I would get back to school from lunch in time to take part in important to me noontime playground activities. In the second grade, I was shoved while playing touch tag on the playground and was pushed so that I fell head first against the concrete edge of the brick school building. With my forehead cut wide open, blood streaming down and my dirty cotton glove (worn partly to keep from getting too cold and partly to keep from getting too dirty) pressed against the cut, I struggled past wide-eyed kids to the wash area.

The wash area had high school girls helping with the mob of kids needing washing up from playing on the dirty school ground. The girls got a hold of my parents and they quickly came and took me to the doctor's office. The doctor looked at the cut and decided to "clamp it shut" instead of stitches that might leave scars. A big, wide, white tape and gauze bandage was added and, of course, I was taken right back to school for afternoon classes. I did get some real attention stares when I entered the classroom with the bandaged up head.

It was also in the first couple of grades I dispensed with measles, chicken pox and multiple bouts with coughing, one of which was finally called the whooping cough. The medical doctor made house calls (even though his office was only a few blocks away and up a flight of stairs). This might have been a good idea to keep me from infecting others and to drive home the point that I was supposed to stay in bed. I liked our family doctor. First, he did not believe in laxatives – so much for the dreaded Agarol and Milk of Magnesia. He did once prescribe some kind of gooey "tonic" that was not very good. What I really liked was he always said "plenty of liquids" and I would get all the ice cold Coke drinks I wanted.

I don't remember being very interested in eating. One time I tried to pour my glass of milk down the kitchen sink. I, of course, got caught and was told in no uncertain terms that one time was enough of that trick. You can get in a lot of trouble doing something this bad. Besides always drinking our milk, we were taught the usual rules to not waste anything and always eat all the food off our plates (someone was always starving somewhere). I tried multiple, multiple times the "I'm not feeling well" line before being sent off to school. My mother would put her hand on my forehead and say, "You don't have a fever." That would always signal the end of the conversation and off to school I would have to go.

I was jealous of my little brother who did not yet have to go to school. I remember having some paper Navy warplanes that were stuffed with cotton to give them some substance. I was aghast one day when I came home and my little brother had torn the paper airplane all apart to get some of the cotton out of it. I quickly and loudly complained to my mother. I think she said something unsym-pathetic to the effect that "I should have put them up." Reeling from such a show of non-compassion, I started my climbing career to the top shelves of the closet to hide all toys of importance.

I walked to the public library. The library was located on the opposite corner across from the gym. I liked getting and reading books. The library, although small, had large wide steps up to the entrance door and tall ceilings inside. It seemed like a big place to me. It was there I really learned a valuable early lesson. While getting some books, I decided the long row of books on the second shelf (top shelf to someone my size) needed straightening up. Kids like myself had put the books back at all different angles. So I proceeded to push on one end of the books to straighten up the books. The push must have been of good force. The next thing I knew there were dozens and dozens of books tumbling off the shelf down to the floor. The commotion caused quite a stir and the librarian was there in a flash. When I arrived home, I was very surprised that my mother knew all about the incident. I was becoming convinced in a big way that I was not about to get away with anything. Of course, I have since pieced together that a hyper, strung out librarian must have been on the telephone to my mother. I also learned from this incident another life lesson. You can also get into a lot of Trouble (with a capital T) by trying to do something good.

Once in a great while we went to the movies. The damp, cold, much advertised, drafty air conditioning made a real difference in the summer. I learned to spell and print my first word by going to the movies. Maybe because the movie was not too interesting, I became fascinated by the two red signs on either side of the movie screen. They stayed on all the time and read "EXIT." After getting home I began printing wherever and on whatever I could "EXIT."

The Methodist Church we attended was located directly across from the gym. We did not walk to the church on Sunday. My dad (my mother did not drive) dropped my brother and me off on Sunday morning for Sunday School. I guess you could say we became the church's problem. The Sunday School teacher was the Clinton mayor's wife, but the mayor didn't attend church. It seemed like many did not attend church other than when the Christmas program was presented. The children's class area was in the basement and had a long sandbox filled with white sand. We were not supposed to get any of the sand on the floor, but I think we managed to do it. I must have attended fairly regular, as I have some attendance awards. I don't remember much about the church, but I probably learned more there than I was aware of. We were taught the Bible and scripture memory. In particular, the 23 Psalm was emphasized and memorized.

The Lord is my shepard; I shall not want.

He maketh me to lie down in green pastures: he leadeth me beside still waters.

He restoreth my soul: he leadeth me in the paths of righteousness for his name's sake.

Yea, though I walk through the valley of the shadow death, I will fear no evil: for thou art with me; thy rod and thy staff they comfort me.

Thou preparest a table before me in the presence of mine enemies: thou anointest my head with oil; my cup runneth over.

Surely goodness and mercy shall follow me all the days of my life: and I will dwell in the house of the Lord for ever.

Psalm 23 Verses 1-6 (KJV)

Methodist Church – 1915 Historical Site

Someone, I suspect the Gideons, passed out pocket-sized bibles at Central Grade School when I was in the third grade and, being a regular reader, I remember reading some of it. I really did not like the children's special programs presented by the church. Usually some sort of performance was required and a costume added for insult. Once I was left as the only Shepard who showed up for the Christmas program and had to sing something alone (it was awful for me and everyone else). I did not appear destined (or encouraged) for show business of any kind. The dreaded participation experiences in the Christmas programs were partly offset by the anticipated appearance of good ole Santa Claus in the basement of the church with our cellophane wrapped gift of hard candy, orange, apple and nuts - all stuck together. My brother and I went to another church for Vacation Bible School in the summer. Here we did various projects. The older boys got to do carpentry projects – such as nailing two empty sewing thread spindles to a block of wood for hanging up a broom. It was one of these times my brother and I were greatly embarrassed. Somehow we got the days mixed up for the Vacation Bible School picnic. When we showed up for with our brown paper bags, the other kids quickly and correctly surmised we had our lunch in those brown bags. Fortunately, one of the older kids with a bicycle, who was the son of one of the men who worked with my dad, quickly said, "I will take those lunch bags back home for you." When we got home that day we had our own little picnic consisting of the fried baloney sandwiches with mustard. It turned out all right.

Music was a required course of study in grade school. I was not what you would call a music talent. The "music room" and piano were located in the basement of Central Grade School. Anytime the school district music leader would test our voices at Central Grade School, I would get moved to the second row. Do-re-mi-fa-so-la-ti-do. As soon as he left, the music teacher would quickly move me back to the first row. The first row was *not to sing*. I could not even sing "Up on the housetop reindeers paused, out jumped good ole Santa Claus…".

Fortunately, I was also excused from any music performances.

Our grade school report cards were regular, noteworthy events. They were to be carried home and then returned signed by one of our parents. School report cards were updated every six weeks including final exam records at the end of 18 weeks. The school report cards were my parents' records of my education (although I think my mom somehow knew everything that was going on). At the top of the cards were grades for Conduct and Effort. It was not good to come home with bad "grades" in these areas. I really liked my first grade teacher, pretty much liked my second grade teacher, but thought my third grade teacher was more than a bit "tyrannical." It was bad timing to have a tyrannical teacher for the third grade because that was when the multiplication tables were taught (or perhaps thinking further, such a teacher was needed for the correct end results). Also I think I developed my hatred of going up to the blackboard during this year. My conduct went from A to B over the three years and effort slipped to C in the third grade. Next were the records of Days Absent and Days Tardy. Even with all my sickness in the second grade I only missed eight and one half days of school. In the third grade, although I really did not feel well, thanks to my mom I missed zero days. Next were the subject grades. In the first year Arithmetic, Art, English, Music, Reading, Spelling and Writing were taught. In the second year English was not taught. And in the third year English was again taught and Health was added. Since I got C's in Music, that must have been the lowest grade given. It was probably here I first became not too concerned about grades. As printing became writing, my writing grades slipped toward C. Otherwise it was an up/down A-B performance. Each year when I graduated, as a reward I was able to go to the large 5&10 cent store on Main Street and spend some money for a toy or game. It was really great to be out of school for the summer.

Once when a nephew on my mother's side came to town in the summer, I went with him to the 5&10 cent store. When passing the toy counter, I asked him if he would buy a little set of play tools for me. He did buy them for me and, when we got home with them, my mother was horrified. I found out this was a big no-no to be asking others for something (especially something I could do without).

My first basketball memory was being taken to games sometime before the 3rd grade. My father followed basketball and the local team was very good that year. The gym was an exciting place to me. People yelled there and nobody in particular seemed to be doing anything bad. It was a place where some people became very animated. The two hand set shot and the underhanded free throw were popular. Players were not wimps. When a timeout was taken they would huddle together on the floor. There was no running over and gathering around the coaches. A basket on wheels with towels would be shoved out to the huddled players. When the timeout was over, the basket would be shoved back across the floor to the bench. When I got home, we didn't have any basketballs or nets, but my younger brother and I found a box and some rags. We would pretend timeouts, shuttling the basket across the floor.

Sometime during this time period my father won a major prize like the father in *The Christmas Story*. His major prize was also fragile. Evidently my father took part in the only form of legal gambling available in Indiana at the time consisting of punchboards at wayside cafes. These were boards that a little punch was used to push small papers out the back. The small papers indicated whether you won or you lost (mostly lost of course). The winning major prize my father brought proudly home was a pair of lamps, each with a large glass dice as the base. As I recall my mother's reaction was similar to *The Christmas Story* movie mom. After a short time the lamps could be found in the basement and from there they disappeared.

Grandpa and Grandma

My Grandfather the Blacksmith

Our Grandma and Grandpa on my father's side lived in the small town of Marshall, which was in Parke County. We went east from Clinton, across the Wabash River Bridge, left at the Lyford Y, onto a section of the famous, two lane US 41 - Chicago to Florida highway. This two-lane highway followed numerous curves around and up and down the hills of Parke County to first reach Rockville and then a few miles on to the turnoff to Marshall. The two lane road into Marshall ran parallel to a railroad track. Reaching Marshall we made a right turn, crossed the railroad tracks, drove under an arch over the road that had the letters MARSHALL and past the Kraft cheese factory a few blocks; then we turned right again down a street path that dead ended at Grandpa and Grandma's house. Grandfather was still working as a blacksmith. He fixed and sharpened saws and farm implements. He also held various other jobs. One of these other jobs was working sometimes at the local slaughterhouse. On his property was a barn like structure with the blacksmith hearth and some belt driven machines. Their property was mainly a hobby farm. My brother and I liked to go there. There were fruit trees – peach, red apple, yellow apple, green apple, cherry, plum, persimmon and pear. There were berries – strawberry, blackberry, black raspberry and red raspberry. There were red tomatoes, yellow tomatoes, spinach, asparagus, white radishes, red radishes, corn, carrots, green beans, peas, red peppers, yellow peppers, green peppers, squash, eggplant, lettuce, cabbage, onions, cucumbers, green grapes, purple grapes, muskmelons, watermelons, potatoes and sweet potatoes. We had a good time picking and eating. The old farmhouse had a large kitchen, small living room and small bedroom. My grandmother did quilting and the large wooden quilt frame was in the bedroom. During the war, the house had oil wick lamps for lighting. Later Grandpa got a raft of batteries with a generator to charge them up for lighting, until the REA (Rural Electrification Act) provided electric power after the war. The yard in front of the house was a nice small, elongated, football field shape for my brother and I to play football. The football games would sometimes be interrupted so we could watch the steam locomotives. The railroad grade into Marshall was enough of a challenge that it was exciting to watch the coal burning steam trains chug up and down the grade. The house was heated by a large coal burning stove in the living room. In the real cold weather, after we played outside, an extra treat was Grandpa digging out the popcorn and a wire shaker basket with a wire lid on a long handle. We would then pop the popcorn by shoving and shaking the wire basket with corn kernels through the open door of the coal stove. Melted butter and salt galore would then be added. If we got there for Sunday dinner, Grandpa raised chickens and after "wringing a chicken's neck", we had chicken for dinner. Maybe it was the reason I was small, but I used to eat the neck piece of the chicken. Also I liked pickled pigs feet and even ate hominy at this time. I never, however, ate large quantities of any of these foods. Then there were the outhouse adventures. The only water plumbing to be had was the outside well pump. It was a real education for us. There was the Montgomery Ward catalog for toilet paper and in the summer some of the biggest flies I have ever seen. You didn't have to tell me to get a move on for the winter trips to the outhouse.

My Proud Grandmothers

During the war the highway speed limit was 35 MPH and the bad part of going to Marshall, really only a few miles away, was the time it seemed to take. Even after the war the trip was slow with the curves, hills and traffic on US 41. To my brother and I it was a very long trip. Gas rationing during the war cut down on the number of trips. Sometimes there were good radio programs, like Jack Benny, Fibber McGee and Molly, Fred Allen, the Amateur Hour, the Quiz Kids, Lone Ranger, Baby Snooks, etc., to listen to on the way. Of course, my brother and I had the imaginary line across the back seat. My parents were born too soon to have cars with a wonderful seatbelt for children in the backseat. However, they did know how to apply the hand of discipline to the seat of knowledge. Once a summer we would all meet at Rockville, the county seat of Parke County, where the courthouse was surrounded on all four sides by stores. The Parke County Fair would be setup in the streets around the courthouse. It would be an opportunity to exchange some of the harvest from the hobby farm and meet some other relatives. My brother and I got to ride the rides and eat the food. In the summertime, we sometimes would stop at the Rockville city park. It had a large "3 dip" slide. The only time my Grandparents came all the way to Clinton was Christmas day. Our Christmas was much like *The Christmas Story.* Some exceptions were my father was a gooseberry pie and horehound candy connoisseur and we never ate out no matter what the tragedy.

The two lane roads that were the norm of the day ran right alongside farmers' fences. PHD's (Post Hole Diggers) had preceded us along the roadsides, installing the well known sequential Burma-Shave shaving cream signs. These clever advertising signs were a big hit. The signs were spaced one after another, in must read fashion.

ONE BURMA-SHAVE

THE SCHOOL KID CRIED

AT LEAST I'LL SMELL

AS IF I TRIED

BURMA-SHAVE

My other Grandmother lived in Cloverdale (my mother's father had died when she was in high school). Grandmother only came to Clinton one time and stayed for a week. This was the week I had my tonsils taken out. For this operation, we went to Terre Haute to a doctor's office up a flight of stairs. I was put to sleep using ether and when I woke up the tonsils were gone and we went home in the afternoon. Doctors later told me that part of my palate was also gone, something that has never bothered me (no harm no foul?). I was given special treatment that week with all the ice cream I wanted. The trip to visit Grandmother in Cloverdale was even further and slower. It took a couple of hours and was about 70 miles. This trip consisted of turning the other direction at the Lyford "Y" (about 1 mile east of Clinton) and taking US 41 south to Terre Haute. Terre Haute was the big city to us with a population of around 65,000. It was the closest big time shopping alternative to Chicago (North), St Louis (West), Indianapolis (East) and Evansville (South). It had Alden's, Meis and Root's department stores. It had Kresge, McCrory and Woolworth dime stores. And not to be over-looked were the Indiana and Grand theatres and the Terre Haute House and Deming Hotels. It was home to Indiana State Teachers College, Rose Polytechnic Institute, Deming Park and the Three-I minor league baseball team. We always took the bypass around to the east of Terre Haute using Fruitridge Avenue. A landmark was the Ann Page Foods factory. Fruitridge Avenue went through a couple of railroad yards and whether the bypass would really save time was always a risky decision. The Pennsylvania and New York Central railroads went through Terre Haute. Crossing the numerous railroad tracks also seemed really dangerous.

I remember seeing a movie as a child where someone crossing the railroad tracks got their foot caught in a railroad switch and ended up run over by a locomotive freight train. The visual of being plastered up against the front of that train was very vivid to me. Once I had been asked for some reason to go from Main Street to my father's place of work on Water Street. It was only about a block, but required crossing the railroad tracks. As I proceeded across the tracks, after carefully looking both ways, twice and then some, a siren (that was unbeknownst to me located close by) sounded full blast. I was confused – I had looked both ways, something was right upon me – the adrenalin spike must have been past all limits. I moved fast, plenty fast, as fast as my laggard legs would follow my brain commands to get off the railroad tracks. After running about

100 feet, well past the railroad tracks, I began to figure out what had happened. The town siren had gone off, up close and very personal, on one of its regular test cycles. While I was concentrating about watching for trains, it got my full and immediate attention. I was very respectful of railroad tracks and trains.

After the crossing all the Terre Haute railroad yards, we turned east on US 40 toward Indianapolis. This took us through another dangerous area. The Federal Penitentiary was located off US 40 and signs were posted not to pick up hitchhikers - no way. I could not think of anything much worse than getting caught doing something very bad, much less ending up in the penitentiary. We turned off US 40 to the south to Cloverdale. My Grandmother lived with my aunt and uncle on a farm located on the other side of Cloverdale. Compared to the Marshall farm, which was more of a hobby farm, this was a real farm. I always thought it would have been much more exciting to have lived on a farm. This was not particularly because of animals. I was not too fond of animals. When the photographer with the pony came by our house for pictures, I said no way. There is a picture of my little brother on the pony. I liked the wide open spaces, fields of corn, sheds, barns, creeks, trees, weeds, etc.

I always thought I could have made a small, inside basketball gym in a barn loft. That would have been the ultimate. My aunt would take my brother and I on the farm chores. There was the barn where cattle needed hay from the loft. There was the long chicken house with hundreds of chickens being raised for market and needing feed. One of the best "toys" we ever had was to bring home empty boxes used to transport the baby chicks. My brother and I used these in the basement to make numerous houses, caves, forts, garages, etc. There was also the fun of gathering eggs. Sometimes we got to take one of the big shovels and slide corn into a hole in the floor to a corn shucker machine that was used to grind corn into corn feed. We were very careful not to get too close to the hole in the floor or let go of the shovel. They had turkeys in a field with high fences, but turkeys were a different size and a different story than chickens. We left the turkeys alone. Walking trips down the gravel country road often would give the opportunity to throw rocks at snakes and run. The farm even had a mini junkyard and my brother and I could climb on an old tractor or truck and pretend to drive it. Once another uncle visited and he told us, as I recall, to go looking in the garden bean patch for something big. Sure enough we found a hugh watermelon there. Since the trip was so long, dad would stop at the drugstore and get the Sunday paper before starting the trip. I liked to read the comics and sports. I always looked at all the pictures in the sports section on the way. When we got to Cloverdale, my dad and uncle as an extra treat would go into town to a magazine store. There my brother and I would get to pick out a comic book for our reading education. My uncle used to say, "I thought those were comic books but I never see you laughing when you read them." If the weather was hot and we needed to get some gas, we would stop and get a soda from the metal icebox containers. Since the glass bottles were sitting in ice water, they always tasted real cold and extra special. Being only six ounces, the drink did not last very long and we needed to leave the empty bottle behind. My brother remembers the time he decided to be the man putting gas in the tank. Dad was quite upset when he found out the pretend gas was dirt and rocks. Fortunately, I think the "pretend gas" was primarily big rocks and the only long lasting effect was a tank that would forever contain less gasoline. Once or twice for some reason we would stay overnight. I remember having big, feather pillows, and my brother and I having a fine time pillow fighting. The end result of that was not good for me as I had a badly stopped-up head and runny nose for several days afterward. Here for Sunday dinner it once again was chicken and my aunt did the neck twisting job on

the chicken. Mashed potatoes and gravy were always included. I

would shape the potatoes like a volcano and pour the gravy in the

center cavity. The dinner was usually topped off with hot peach

cobbler and vanilla ice cream. Grandma always kept a glass jar

with peppermints in her room. My brother and I made sure we vis-

ited the jar during the visit. The trip back home was usually in the

dark, making the penitentiary and train yard even more ominous.

The Burma-Shave signs were harder to read at night.

HER CHARIOT

RACED AT 80 PER

THEY HAULED AWAY

WHAT HAD

BEN HUR

BURMA-SHAVE

Grades 4-6

I remember during the war that stars were hung in the windows of the homes of those who had someone in the service. There were many sad separations in town. Downtown against the outside wall of the JCPenny store was a large billboard with the names of those serving in the wars. A star next to the name sadly indicated they would not be coming back. My father was exempted from military service for being in a critical industry. After graduating with a bachelor of science degree in electrical engineering from Purdue in 1932, he found there were no jobs for graduates because of the Great Depression. Somehow my Grandpa as a blacksmith had managed to send his two sons to college. My dad's older brother graduated with a music degree from Indiana University and became a college professor of music.

My Father the Engineer

My dad had met my mom on a blind date while he was still in college. My mother was from Spencer (about a 100 miles from West Lafayette and 40 or so miles from Bridgeton where my Grandparents had returned to). Mom lived on a farm outside of Spencer. She was a "trailing" child. She was born when my Grandmother was 45 years old and had one older brother and two older sisters. Mom was known as the "spoiled child" by her siblings. Her father died while she was in high school. I can remember my Grandfather on my father's side saying that dad was always going "down there" to see her. They were married in Vincennes and had a short honeymoon at French Lick in April of 1933. Dad still had no job, so they lived for a while on the farm with my Grandmother and one of mom's older sisters. Finally, dad got a job working in an icehouse operated by the electric power company. After living in the French Lick – West Baden area, they moved to Kokomo. When I was born he was listed as a Substation Operator. As economic times got better, he was able to move into an electrical engineering job. It was the power company engineering job that was considered a critical industry position. My father's wages were frozen for the four years of the war. My father would tune in the radio for the war news every day after lunch before heading back to work. I remember the honking of horns and celebration announcing the victory in Europe. The end of the war brought uncertainty for the economic future for the area. What would provide jobs replacing the war industries? Many workers and their families would probably have to move away from the area. The end of this war also meant the end of "frozen housing" and that resulted in the fact that our rental house could be and was sold. When the house was "sold out from under us," we got an eviction notice. I recall our family looking for a place to live and for the money to buy it as traumatic events. Both houses and money were hard to find. I was with my mother once when she gave someone a "piece of her mind" about the situation. We ended up with what was called a "school loan" for $1,200 and bought two houses, two sheds and an outhouse located on a small corner lot. Thankfully, the main house had been recently "upgraded" to indoor plumbing. The house was located on the other end of Ninth Street from Little Italy. The move was during the summer between the third and fourth grades.

My Mother the Homemaker

Sports really entered my life when we moved to the new house in 1945. I had played no sports at all up to this time. The new house was located at the edge of town close to the city park. In fact, our house sat on the corner of the oiled dirt road that led to the city park. The park contained the Clinton High School football stadium, a baseball field, a somewhat shabby park area with swings, picnic shelter house, teeter-totters, slides, etc., and a rundown set of dirt surface tennis courts. The baseball field had screened, covered wooden stands behind home plate and a small concessions stand. There were no fences around the baseball ballpark. A chalkboard, inning-by-inning scoreboard was located across from first base, sitting up on a hill. The football stadium was enclosed by a wooden fence with barbed wire on top. The stadium had wooden stands on both sides and the seating capacity was somewhat oversized at this time. The stadium was originally built in the coal mining boom years, when Clinton was over twice the current population and had rugged football teams made up of coal miners' sons. Beyond the park was a strip mine area that was responsible for the dynamite blasting that rocked the house, the constant steam shovel noise that floated through the windows and the single railroad track with its associated coal cars and trains. Fortunately over a short time period the coal mining activity moved further and further away from our house. Shortly after moving, a new neighbor came running down the street yelling, "Victory in Japan, victory in Japan, the war is over, the war is over!!" I remember the *Life Magazine* pictures that told of the "A Bomb" that had been developed and used to end the war.

Times were now really due for a change. Everyone was driving at least a four-year-old car. Public and private capital improvements had been postponed for years. Perhaps now our 1936 Ford could be replaced (although there was still a small matter of having available cars and enough money to pay for them). Priority would now shift from the all out effort to build up the military to more peaceful purposes. There were sure some happy reunions when our victorious troops came home to stay and families joyfully celebrated.

Our new home's lot size was small. When the purchase was made the lot had a four room house at the front, another smaller house just behind it, with the two sheds and an outhouse at the rear. The front house, even though upgraded to indoor plumbing, needed much work. The interior walls consisted of small wooden lathes covered with plaster. Many layers of old wallpaper had been applied to the walls. Heat was provided by a coal cooking stove in the kitchen. Four of us and one bedroom was not going to be workable over the long haul. My brother and I moved into the bedroom and my parents took the dining room. There was no thought of having work done by someone else. First of all my father was an engineer and second there was no money. The fix-up activity got off to a very bad start when the wooden ladder that was left with the house collapsed with a bang and dumped my father to the floor. Fortunately he was only shaken up and not hurt. A steamer was used to remove the wallpaper. Steaming wallpaper was an operation I was told to stay out of the way of. After the wallpaper was removed, the walls with cracked plaster were repaired and painted. The kitchen stove was soon replaced by a coal furnace located in the basement (this furnace was later converted to oil). The old wooden sash windows with ropes tied to weights in the walls were refinished. A new shingle roof was required. A new front porch was going to be required.

Our Little House on the Corner

Over the next few years, my father reworked the house and added a kitchen and back porch using the lumber salvaged from the sheds and part of the torn down second house. The new plywood kitchen cabinets were all made with a handsaw. It was quite a project, but my father kept right at it (except for the summer he got very sick with pneumonia from all the house building activity). When the expansion to the house was finished, my brother and I moved to where the kitchen had been and my parents to the bedroom. We had plenty of kitchen cabinet shelf space in our bedroom. The mostly torn down second house was converted into a single car garage. I got to help tear down these buildings. It was great fun to bust off the plaster and crow bar the lathe boards off the walls. I was not much help putting anything back. The yard was small and partly hilly. The really tough part about maintaining the yard was that the lawn mower was a dull blade, push mower and the grass was crabgrass. The crabgrass cut like wire in the fall. We would not have considered fertilizing this grass (making grass grow was not considered remotely desirable). I don't remember being asked to mow the yard, but it seemed the thing to do to help out. It gave me something to do and a sense of accomplishment.

With the move to Ninth Street my brother and I were supposed to transfer from Central Grade School to South Grade School. My brother was just starting school. We had a neighbor boy we played with all the time and we were looking forward to going to the new school with him. It was quite a walk to this new school. I'm not sure about my brother, but I didn't seem to get along well at this school. Part of it might have been that I was the new kid on the block. Part of it might have been the sterner teacher. Part of it might have been the class requiring a sterner teacher. At any rate and I'm not sure how it happened, but my father was able to get us transferred back into the old Central Grade School and there I had a good teacher and class situation. My father was able to do this because we were very close to the school boundary line, the school was on his way to and from work, and I think he knew the school superintendent. I was really grateful for the change. Now we usually got a ride to school as it was on the way to my father's work. However, I some-times walked home for lunch and always walked home after school. Sometimes, at noon I would run home from school, Third Street to Ninth Street, in a race to beat the kids that had bicycles. I was small but had good speed. Trips to the library were now further and more difficult, but the getting and reading of books went on.

The radio introduced us to major league baseball -- the "Cubs" and "Cardinals." The town had split allegiance with Chicago and St. Louis being about equally accessible. We got to listen at school to the last game of the 1945 World Series, when the Cubs and Tigers played because our teacher was an avid Cubs fan. I followed her lead and became a Cubs fan. It was not a happy day, as the Cubs were badly beaten. I would listen to the Cubs' Wrigley Field home games during the day and sometimes the Cardinals' games. The listening problem was that the AM radio was mostly static in the summer and I could barely hear WIND Chicago. I still remember the broadcasts starting with the announcement that "It's a beautiful day in Chicago." It was a beautiful day any day we could play baseball. Our backyard became a pretend major league ballpark. The rear wire fence formed left and left center. There was a break in the fence in the middle where the outhouse used to be. One end of the fence made a right angle turn to form left field and the other end connected at right angle with a low concrete wall forming the right field wall. A tennis ball became the game ball. The person at bat stood up by the house and threw high fly balls. The fence would be covered by sweet pea vines in the summer. The ball had to be thrown very high, because a home run had to be catchable, clearing the fence and either touch a sweet pea vine or fall within three feet

of the fence. Hence, we would constantly go back to the vines for

spectacular Wrigley Field catches or Harry Carey "Holy Cow" home

runs. Harry Carey was the announcer for the archrival Cardinals.

Infield was practiced alone by throwing tennis balls for hours at a

time against the garage and throwing out runners by hitting a spe-

cial spot on the side of the garage.

My Brother's Convertible Cart

My summers were spent outdoors. Actually inside the house

was similar to being outdoors. All the windows would be open and

the screen doors in place. The only relief from the heat was an eight-inch oscillating fan that was usually located in the middle of the living room floor. The fan essentially just blew the heat around. A breezy night would not be so bad. We had a large cottonwood tree across the street. The tree had large leaves and would make a rustling sound with the wind. In the fall the large, dry leaves could be heard being moved around the street and sidewalk by the wind. I spent many hours playing baseball and dreamed of becoming a major league baseball player. When I could get a hold of a copy of the *Sporting News*, I would read it from cover to cover. Anytime there was activity at the ballpark, I would be down there to see it. These were strictly my ideas; I did not get encouragement from any-where. There was no such thing as organized kids' baseball. I had never played baseball before the fourth grade. We only had pick-up games and chose up sides. I was fortunate. I got to know every-one on my side of town who was playing baseball and most of them were older. There were seldom enough kids to have two full teams so I would get to play with the high school players by usually filling in at the right field or second base position. Although small, I could wield a mean Ted Williams 32 inch bat. I was allowed to play more often after surprising infielders with a line shot past them before they could react. Between meals it was out the screen door and off to the ballpark. At grade school we did play some softball and for a couple of games played other teams. Once we were given some game t-shirts and ball caps. The marbles were replaced by softball, dodge tag and football on the schoolhouse playground. One of my birthday gifts was a softball bat. For baseball bats we sawed off the broken ends of bats thrown away by teams playing at the ballpark. Sometimes the whole broken bat could be salvaged by wrapping friction tape around the broken section.

Always being down at the baseball park, I would often shag fly balls for whoever was practicing hitting. Once I remember there were a lot of grown ups standing around and as a line drive came at me I heard shouting, "you got it, you got it, you got it". Well, I did have it, but it is amazing to me how that little bit of encouragement from a stranger has stayed with me. You might call it an insignificant event with significance. I wonder how insignificant events add up to great significance. I especially wonder this when many what are called really significant events do not seem to add up at all.

Part of the strip mine had been turned into a dumpsite. Here was a great place to play and shoot the Red Ryder beebee guns.

The objective was usually to sink anything we could find that would float. When the beebees ran out or the sinking progress seemed too slow, it was time to throw bricks and cement blocks creating as big a splash as possible. A large glass Purex bottle was a prize find for a target to sink.

In the fall there was too much excitement at the football stadium to stay away, although sometimes we waited so that we got in free when they quit selling tickets at halftime. It started out as pretty nice evening weather in the fall, but going to the games got down-right cold by November. I don't remember ever buying anything at the games. The next day after a game my brother and I would scout around the stadium looking for what had been left behind. We found a purse once and turned it in, but found very little rubbish of interest. An empty tobacco can was a real find. My brother and I messed around with football, but I was always too small and my mom would hear nothing of it. I was not about to get hurt was her viewpoint. For a while we had to make do with oatmeal containers as footballs. One bad mistake, like falling on the "ball," could ruin the game. This was eventually replaced by a miniature play football and later by the real thing.

Golf became another available sport. We obtained a broken golf club and found a couple of golf balls to use. We went to the park and buried empty soup cans in the ground for holes, laying out a golf course. One day a neighbor saw what we were doing and gave us a couple of old, wooden shaft golf clubs to use. These clubs stood up pretty well for us. The golf course was so short we never tried to "kill" the ball. One nice part of this sport activity was that I could play a round of golf alone when no one was around to play with. We also found an old tennis racquet left from dad's college days and tried some tennis. There was no playing tennis alone.

A makeshift wood plywood backboard, painted white, and a basketball goal with a net were mounted first on a pole and then shifted to the side of the single garage made from the converted house. With the roof overhang eve, a small drive under area was provided. The court was the hard ground that part of the old house had covered and little grass tried to grow there. Many hours were spent bouncing the basketball and shooting baskets. It became more difficult to shoot baskets in the winter, but it was not impossible. In fact, when ice formed on the ground (typical central Indiana winter weather is below freezing at night and slightly above freezing in the afternoon) a smooth ice surface would form over the usually uneven ground. After spreading some readily available coal ashes on the ice, a level, better-than-dirt court was made. The "better" court did have some drawbacks. As the ice surface melted, the basketball and our hands became caked with wet ash and dirt. Still it was a small price to pay when a person wanted desperately to play basketball. The white backboard also suffered, turning brown from the wet ash and dirt. Once I ran out the basement door, dribbled out to the court, leaped up in the air to fire off a one hand jumper, and then was surprised to feel my feet fly straight up. I landed square on the small of my back. It completely knocked the breath out of me. I don't know how long I lay there moaning and groaning before being able to hobble up to my feet again. The lesson I learned and didn't forget was to put ashes down first and shoot jump shots second.

Inside in a little basement room, my brother and I mounted a coffee can for a basket and the good ol' tennis ball became the basketball. This allowed for some indoor poor man's basketball games. I was also given a basketball game that had flippers to shoot a ping-pong ball at baskets. When the ping-pong ball was flipped it would either make a basket or miss and then roll around into a hole in the court. Under each hole were flippers to begin the sequence all over. It was designed with flippers so that a person on each side of the court could play against each other. Cardboard scoreboards were at each end. However, not having anyone else to play with much of the time, I would play with this for hours, operating the flippers for both sides. I would set up tournaments and play for championships. This worked pretty well, since a missed or made basket would bounce onto the court and roll around until it would end up in a hole to be flipped by one of the teams. I must have driven my parents crazy with the endless sound of the ping-pong ball being flipped around. It was one gift I imagine they would have liked to have taken back.

I attended a few high school basketball games with my parents. Clinton's archrival was the Terre Haute Garfield Purple Eagles. Garfield was located on the North side of Terre Haute, closest to Clinton. During this period Clinton had its best team the same year Garfield had a great team. During the year, Clinton played Garfield, away and home, at the beginning and end of the regular season basketball schedule. Garfield was undefeated at the last regular season game. Hopes were high for a big Clinton upset. One might sell one's soul for a victory here – this victory surely being worth more than a pot of soup. However, when I saw Garfield's 6' 11" center duck his head and shoulders around the door jam to get onto the court I said, "Oh-oh." Clinton did not even come close to winning this must-win big game. Clinton finished the year with a 20-6 record. The Clinton Wildcats went all the way to the Semifinals in Indianapolis where they lost to Shelbyville, the eventual state champion.

Garfield created a lot of excitement by completing an undefeated season and was favored to win the Indiana State Championship. No Indiana team had ever gone undefeated and won the Indiana State Title. The Garfield Purple Eagles went undefeated all the way to Indianapolis and to the final game. They played for *all the marbles* and lost the championship game to Shelbyville. A crushing defeat ended what until then had been a perfect season; I hated to lose even one marble!

Geography and History got added to the subject list in the fourth grade. Geography was my favorite study. I was able to make the

Honorable Mention Lists, but continued the C in Music and Writing.

Also my Art grade had fallen over the years from A to C.

I was the smallest boy in the sixth grade and only two girls were

smaller. I measured my height often against marks on a doorframe.

I was really concerned about never getting tall. Part of the problem

was probably my birthday, as some in the class were up to a year

older. I had discovered girls. I had discovered the movies. Putting

the two together I asked a girl to the movies in the sixth grade, and

then wondered why it caused so much excitement. She never said

yes or no. I think I picked the tallest girl in the class, which wasn't

too bright. I remember I asked her in the coat hall, where a lot of

mischievous action was always going on. The blond, cute, smiley-

faced girl I really wanted to ask came by my desk and whispered

"shame on you." All this set my confidence back years. Movies

were 35 cents at the two main theatres in town – the Palace and the

Wabash. The cost of admission might have posed a problem, but I

thought I could solve that one. Movies were even cheaper on Ninth

Street in Little Italy at an old rundown theatre named the Columbia

Theatre. At the Columbia you could hear the rats or mice scurrying

on the floor for dropped popcorn. We used to ask to purchase the unpopped grits. The grits were screened out of the popcorn machine to a drawer underneath the popcorn popper. I think we paid a nickel for a sack of popcorn kernel grits. The paper bag would be full and quite heavy. The popcorn grease soaked the paper and made it somewhat disintegrate in our hands. The bag of kernel grits lasted for the whole show with often some left over to take home. What a deal! Needless to say, this theatre did not show first release features and the old "Bowery Boys" movies were our favorites.

I was ready to graduate to the next corner of the school block – the big brick building labeled Clinton Junior High. There was no graduation party or ceremony or even a certificate I can find for getting out of grade school. It was no big deal and evidently the expected activity. I didn't even get the reward of going to the 5 and 10 cent store for a toy or game purchase.

Junior High – Seventh Grade

Getting a bicycle was a big event. My brother and I were late getting them. I don't know if it was the cost, mother not wanting us to get hurt or the idea of keeping us closer to home. All these reasons were probably valid. My brother and I got used bikes. Riding bicycles greatly increased our territory. We could ride to the strip mine, the ballpark, the grocery store, school, library, up the hill past the railroad tracks, through the woods trail roads we made ourselves, across town, up town, etc. I was now in Junior High hitting the big time. I would leap out of bed, down a quick bowl of Wheaties or Cheerios cereal, leap on my bicycle and head out to school. Quickly parking the bike in the rack behind the gym, I would rush up the back outside stairs of the gym. You see, the coach would open the gym for a few minutes before school and using the four practice goals cranked down from the ceiling on the courtsides of the gym, two games could be played at the same time across court. The first kids to get to the gym steps would get to be team captains and get to select other team members as they arrived. It was a very organized, intense, completely unsupervised activity. Once the gym back doors were unlocked by the coach, we would race into the gym, take off our shoes and play in sock feet (no time to change and we did not want to carry around tennis shoes). Thinking back, I have often wished that something could have motivated me the way these early morning basketball sessions did, and been as much fun! The same general thing would happen when the gym was open during lunch. It was harder for me to get involved because I went home for the lunch hour. We never even thought of taking lunch to school because my mom served up three solid meals and expected them to be eaten by the family. There were no school cafeterias and bringing lunch bags was for those out of town bus kids. I still raced home on the bike, ate lunch in big gulps, raced back to school and got into the rotation for the next games (the games had a score limit and the losing team had to give up their place on the court to whatever team that was eagerly waiting).

Early Morning Motivation

It was also in the seventh grade that reading became an even bigger passion. I went through the library reading many books, as well as reading all those we happened to have at home. At home I had the Heratio Alger, Jr. books that had belonged to my father. The Alger books depicted working heros, from rags to riches, and I thought they were great stories. He wrote many books with similar themes: *Julius the Street Boy, The Young Adventurer, Making His Way, The Young Acrobat, Try and Trust, Erie Train Boy, Ragged Dick*, etc. I liked the independent, honest, hard working boys who made their way through trials and troubles to bigger and better lives. I also devoured the sports books by John R Tunis who wrote about Indiana basketball. Tunis was from the eastern part of the United States and, after he visited Indiana, he felt basketball was taken too

63

seriously. People in Indiana seemed to be fanatical about basket-ball according to Tunis. His series of books made me even more exited about basketball. I read many baseball books, too, and the World Series could get my heart beating fast. This was what I want-ed most – to play in the seventh game of the World Series between the National League champions and the American League cham-pions. I read one of the largest books in the library – Jules Verne's *Mysterious Island.* I would sneak-read books after bedtime hours using light from another room or a flashlight under the covers. For some reason I could not get as excited about the required reading books for English. I don't remember any emphasis on reading or reading contests in any grades. Reading was interesting and a fun way to learn.

It was in the seventh grade that Art and Music disappeared from the subject list. This happened none too soon from my viewpoint. English and Reading alternated semesters. Physical Education was added. My main school subject interest became math. It started to come pretty easy for me. I was considered somewhat of a brain by some of the girls and that was powerful, powerful motivation for me. I also had a somewhat unique advantage in that my engineering father was available if I got stuck on some problem. He was not a teacher and not easy to approach. Our sessions together were not always very pleasant. He knew how to get the answers and that was what I was after. Most other subjects required good memory and that is not my gift (although I seem to remember a lot about what happens to me directly). I could usually out work others to get toward the top of the class, but I did not really excel unless math was involved. It turned out math was involved in several subjects.

I thought camping and scouting would have been great, but my parents were not camping-oriented and scout troops were not available. I may not have looked too hard. My brother was later able to do some scouting. I read many books on scouting and got copies of *Boy's Life* from the library. Some of my dad's old books were about boy scouting. I thought getting a boat or canoe and exploring creeks and rivers would be the greatest. I always looked at the run-about boats in the Terre Haute Sears store when we went there. I didn't know anyone who had a boat. There were not any lakes close by. I did not know how to swim and was not encouraged to learn. This was the time of polio. There was a great fear of contracting polio and no one knew what was causing it. I was discouraged from activities such as going to the swimming pool (the main summer at-traction in town) over the fear of polio. Some foods were skipped because of doubts or rumors that they were not good for us or sus-pected of causing polio. My mother did not want us getting polio.

A big event was trading the 1936 Ford in on a new 1949 "Little Plymouth". The "Little Plymouth" – was a smaller, low cost, sloped-back sedan. It wasn't a real fancy car and was mainly developed to be a low cost opportunity, but as you can imagine a few improve-ments had been made in all cars since 1936. This car made it easier to get around and I looked forward to driving this car.

Our New Little Plymouth

THESE SIGNS ARE NOT

FOR LAUGHS ALONE

THE FACE THEY SAVE

MAY BE YOUR OWN

BURMA-SHAVE

The school boy's language stepped it up a notch in Junior High. My parents did not use any swear words and I was not expected to either. This made me more than a "little" different, but I had not heard such words at home or gotten used to speaking them. My Grandparents and relatives also did not use any swear words. The closest was my Grandfather. He told of an experience of checking into an Indianapolis Motel and pulling the sheet back, seeing tons of bedbugs and checking right out of the place. Once in awhile he would exclaim, "**BUGHOUSE.**" My brother and I thought that was pretty funny. Perhaps not being allowed to use "bad language" helped me to realize I could be different and I could resist peer pressure. It certainly made me think twice before speaking and hence may have made me even a better listener.

My parents did have one vice and it was smoking. In a town of drinkers and taverns, they did not drink. They were both very heavy smokers, having started smoking in the Depression, continuing throughout the war and now continuing afterwards. Smoking was the "in thing" to do. It seemed everyone smoked. It was a habit that once started was hard to break. The movies, magazines and later TV were full of people smoking and drinking. Cigarette ads were everywhere. Sample cigarettes were given away on street corners. As far as I know there never was any attempt to stop. They used the popular flip-top lighters filled with lighter fluid. Our little house would be filled with smoke. The sunrays would shine through the heavy smoke and highlight floating household dust. I would get irritated when I would ask my dad a question and he would stop to light up. I was not interested in smoking and resolved not to start.

Basketball Player

I decided to go out for the seventh grade basketball team. There was also a Junior High team, so as I recall, the seventh grade team was like the "B" team of Junior High School. I had never played in an organized basketball game or had any coaching. The Junior High School games were played at night just like the High School games and they were played in the Clinton High School gym. The high school coach was also coaching the Junior High School teams. The first game was a home game in the High School gym. At the last minute of the game (I had not been into the game), the coach called me over and said to report to the scorer's bench. The game was on the line. A basket was needed to win the game. There was a timeout and in the huddle he told me to go stand under the basket and directed that the ball was to be thrown to me. We went out on the court and I got under the basket. The ball came straight to me as directed. I don't know how the coach knew I would be open, but I was!!! I grabbed the ball high over my head and fired the ball up toward the basket. It went up, up, up and over the rim and over the other side rim and down, down, down. **No rim, No net, No basket.** I was stunned. I'm not sure I moved. The game ended with one of our guards dribbling toward the basket.

The locker room scene afterwards was one of disgust. Oddly enough, my teammates were not blaming me for the loss, but blaming themselves for all the missed chances. I don't recall anyone saying anything directly to me. I was still stunned. I hurriedly dressed, slipped out the back door of the gym into the cool night air, hopped on my bike and headed for home. I think my dad was at the game, but I don't recall him saying anything to me. I played very little after that, but I did travel with the team.

Restored Clinton High School Gym

We only went to small schools close by – like Dana, Cayuga, Perrysville, Rosedale and Hillsdale. The most interesting part of playing these teams was their various gym facilities. The Clinton High School team would not play in most of these gyms. All the Parke and Vermillion county teams would have to play Clinton High School in Clinton's gym. Their gyms were called "cracker box gyms" and most larger schools would choose not to get caught playing an away game with the smaller schools that knew how to take advantage of their peculiar home court size and configuration. Many of the smaller school gyms only had a few feet of floor space around the edge of the court and some had very little or no room to drive under the basket. Some had ceilings and lighting that had to be considered when taking a long shot. All the buildings were built before World War II. Many of the gyms only had seating for a few fans. The needed budgets and money were not yet available for upgrading school facilities. Also school consolidation talks had started because of the large cost of upgrading the schools, easier transportation of students and opportunity for larger facilities. Long and difficult political discussions and many school board meetings would be necessary to resolve these kinds of issues. There were many post war expectations and the planning for better and new roads quickly moved to the top of the list. Everyone was getting better cars. Good roads and cars were bound to shrink and ease the travel times to and from school. In Indiana, one thing for sure, the basketball program and the basketball gym had to also be given high priority. Some towns were planning gyms to seat more than the town population.

At one school we dressed in the woodshop class area. In another, where the gym was called "the barn" and looked like a converted barn, we dressed in a small corner room next to the stage area with one large heat register in the center of the room. At another gym, the floor area was recessed, surrounded with concrete walls, with only a few feet of out-of-bounds all the way around the court and the bleacher seats looked down onto the submerged playing floor. There was no chance of fan interference with the submerged, pit-like design. Most of the time we did not have to worry about going out into the cold air after a shower – there were no showers. I remember once sitting in the bleachers watching the other Junior High game when the person sitting a couple of rows ahead looked behind me and said "Come sit down here, Tiny". What proceeded past me was one of the biggest people I had ever seen. I imagine he took three or four seats when he sat down. These gyms would not hold very many "Tinys". Our gym looked like a spacious, modern, giant fieldhouse in comparison to these gyms.

I had started out carrying my tennis shoes, socks, uniform, jock strap and towel all rolled together. My parents bought me a gym bag for Christmas. It was a real surprise and was very different style from the other boys' gym bags (being different was not the in thing). The gym bag had my name hand printed on it. Alas, it turned out that I got very little use of it. The bus trips to the games were new to me and a rollicking good time. The big yellow school buses with seats containing next-to-no-padding, lumbered, bounced and banged along with seemingly little shock absorption. No trip along the narrow, two lane roads, no matter how short, seemed to be over quickly. We sang along the way - "100 bottles of beer on the wall, 100 bottles of beer, ohh-ohh what should happen if one should fall -- 99 bottles of beer on the wall, 99 bottles of beer, ohh-ohh what should happen if one should fall, -- 98 bottles of beer on the wall, 98 bottles of beer, ohh-ohh what should happen if one should fall, -- 97 bottles of beer on the wall, 97 bottles of beer, ohh-ohh.........". This song I could sing and I also could remember the words. Oh, that poor bus driver, how long the trip must have seemed to him!

The High School basketball games became must-see events. The school had an arrangement that if a student sold several season tickets, they would earn a free student pass to all the games. This was the way I got into the games. I was a real Elmer Blurt type of low-pressure salesman. Elmer Blurt was a radio character creation of Al Pierce. The bashful door-to-door salesman Elmer Blurt would "knock, knock" on the prospects door and always quickly follow with the familiar line, "There's nobody at home today, I hope, I hope, I hope." I knew at this early age that sales would never be my career calling. Somehow, with my parents suggesting which of their friends was likely to buy tickets, I got the sales done. Without their help, I probably never would have sold a ticket. They were interested in the money savings.

Our High School team while I was in the seventh grade was not too good, winning only a few games. Their season record was 4 wins and 13 losses. The Wabash Valley tournament was one game and out. There seemed to be no spark at all. Clinton was a member of the Western Indiana Conference. They played Sullivan, Linton, Brazil, and the Terre Haute teams of Garfield, Wiley and Gerstmeyer. They lost all these WIC games. However, we had a dwarf student in my seventh grade class and late in the season he was asked by the coach to become the team mascot. His parents agreed and gave their permission. The dwarf mascot wore a team matching black and gold uniform with the number 13 and partici-pated in the shoot-around before the game and at halftime. He was a big fan and team favorite. The mascot inspired the team.

The Dwarf Mascot Inspired the Team

As the Indiana State Tournament started, I found out that I could also see all the Sectional games free by working during the tournament. The work involved watching the playing teams locker area that had to be shared while the next team got ready for the next game, sweeping the playing floor between games and broom sweeping down the trash from the seats after each session. I can still hear the brooms banging against the bleachers and the trash, mostly consisting of paper cups and official programs, sliding and dropping down to the next level. The usual fan excitement built as the 16 team Clinton Sectional started. Clinton (Wildcats), Rockville (Rox), Bridgeton (Raccoons), Rosedale (Hot Shots), Bloomingdale (Bulldogs), Marshall (Bobcats), Tangier (Tigers), Mecca (Arabs), Dana (Aggies), Cayuga (Indians), Green Township (Aces), Newport (Tigers), Hillsdale (Hilltoppers), Montezuma (Aztecs), St. Bernice (Hornets) and Bellmore - Union Township (Eagles) were poised for the supreme effort. These schools drew students from the likes of Universal, Cunot, Fairview Park, Crompton Hill, Shepardsville, Needmore, Sandytown, etc., typical small town, little more than wide places in the roads of Indiana. The population of Vermillion County was about 20,000 and Parke County was about 16,000. Clinton was the largest town at about 6,500. Rockville, the county seat of Parke County, had a population of about 2,500. Montezuma had about 1,200 and Cayuga about 1,000. Other towns came in at about 900 for Dana, 650 for Newport, 450 for Perrysville, 700 for Rosedale, 400 for Bloomingdale and 400 for Marshall. For these small towns, to win one state tournament Sectional game would be a big event to be remembered and celebrated. An upset win was a dream. Tournament teams were matched by drawing before the tournament started. Who you played was the luck of the draw. A good draw could mean a better chance of getting into the semifinals on Saturday. Four wins in a row were needed to win the 16 team Sectional. Every team played one game. Half the teams were gone after the first round. Only two teams would be left to play the final game.

The school band played for regular home games but not for the state tournament. Seats were at a premium for tournament games. The concessions were located on the visitor's side of the gym next to the stage. A popcorn popper was used to fill the gym with the smell of fresh popcorn. Popcorn was hard to resist (and wasn't resisted). Teachers manned the concessions and tickets stations. Drumstick ice cream was a big seller when the temperature in the gym went up. Pop was served in paper cups. These paper cups were the kind that if you stomped on them correctly would elicit a loud bang.

One game early in the tournament was all but decided with only a few seconds left. The sure winner and leading team took the ball out under the opponent's basket and their player proceeded to throw the ball directly into the hands of an opposition player. The opposition player promptly scored to win the game. I can still remember sitting in the locker room waiting for the coaches to leave long after the game. They were having emotional "if only" discussions. If only, he had thrown the ball to the other end of the court, anywhere but directly to the opposing player. It was a sad defeat. This was a lost opportunity. No tournament advance, no next game, season over and nothing could be done about it.

The pumped, rejuvenated Clinton team, with the emotional lift of the dwarf mascot, easily won three straight over Marshall, Dana and Rockville to get to the Saturday night finals. This was almost as many wins as during the regular season. The finals game was to be against a good Bloomingdale team with a great record. This game would not be easy and the Bloomingdale Bulldogs were highly favored to win. The gym was filled to capacity and beyond far before the game start time. The fire marshal was called out to order aisle space. Indiana State Police were visible at courtside. Fans sat and stood on the stage and in the entrance area. There were obviously two camps – Clinton fans against Bloomingdale and all those other small towns rooting for Bloomingdale. "Two bits, four bits, six bits, a dollar, all for Clinton stand up and holler. Two bits, four bits, six bits, a dollar, all for Bloomingdale stand up and holler. TWO BITS,

FOUR BITS, SIX BITS" --- back and forth it went as the crowd en-

tertained itself with their true convictions. This game was serious

business. The Sectional championship was on the line. This was

the Saturday night event of the year. Parking space was nonex-

istent for blocks around the gym. Everyone knew they needed to

arrive early for this game. The cheering noise was deafening and

there were some real shreaky voices standing out. Cheerleaders

were in constant motion responding to the other teams cheering.

The gym temperature was headed up. I had to watch the game

while standing on a folding chair in the hallway to the Clinton locker

room. It was a very exciting game. Clinton won the Sectional 34-

27; the Sectional title was theirs. The celebration started. Each

member of the team climbed the ladder to cut down the nets. The

Clinton fans were cheering wildly. The mascot was hoisted up to

help cut the nets. How far could they go with their dwarf mascot

and new found winning ways? We would know in just one week.

The basketball season had not ended. Another week was needed

to practice. More pep sessions as an excuse to miss class time.

Clinton was one of the state's elite schools - one out of 64 teams left

in the Indiana State Basketball Tournament. Four seniors on this team still had a shot at more Indiana worship. Oh, to be a real hero. Give me that basketball. We can do it.

The Regionals were next and by the draw the winner of the Clinton Sectional was to play the winner of the Attica Sectional. Attica had also won their Sectional. Attica was a team that had beaten Clinton by 20 plus points during the regular season. Still expectations were high – this was NOT, I repeat NOT the same Clinton team. Many fans made the trip to the Regional. The game was a valiant effort that could have gone either way. Clinton lead in the first quarter 12-9 and at half 20-17. The game was tied 11 times. However, missed free throws in the end doomed the Wildcats. The third quarter and end of the game ended in a tie. In overtime, Clinton fell one point short and with the final score of 43-42, Clinton's season ended. Five Clinton players had played the entire game, with the only substitution coming in overtime when a player fouled out. The Attica Ramblers would continue the tournament quest for this year.

The state tournament went on, of course. The Semifinals were played at Butler University in Indianapolis, Indiana University in

Bloomington, Purdue University in West Lafayette and Muncie Central High School in Muncie. Tickets for the Championship were at a premium. There were 779 schools and 100 of them only got two tickets. Distribution methods were designed to prevent scalping tickets. Jasper from the southern part of the state won the championship. What was surprising was that Jasper entered the tournament with an 11-9 record. They won 10 straight games to get the title. Although anyone can win the tournament, not many teams win the Championship that have nine losses during the season. The last game was a close 62-61 win over Madison. Glory was often won or lost by a single point. "What if, what if" didn't amount to much in a basketball tournament. The losers would be quickly forgotten.

Baseball Student Manager

Maybe because I was always around the ballpark, I really can't remember how or why, but as baseball season started I seemed to have become the student manager for the Clinton High School baseball team. This was great because I got out of the last period of school (typically a study period). I already knew many of the players from the summer pickup games. Since the ballpark was close to the house, being student manager worked out well. The baseball team was senior dominated and these kids knew how to play baseball. The baseball games were played right after school. The bus rides were not as boisterous in the daytime but great events nonetheless. The trips to mostly WIC opponents were much further, but the roads were a little better. The same old, yellow school busses were used. Off we went to the playing fields of the other Western

Indiana Conference teams on the two lane roads.

OTHERS CLAIM

THEIR PRODUCTS GOOD

BUT OURS

DOES WHAT

YOU THINK IT SHOULD

BURMA-SHAVE

The baseball team had good chemistry and spirit. I remember

one game being "bowled over in a cloud of dust." This happened

while I was leaning over straightening the bats and the excited team

suddenly charged out onto the field. I chased down balls, lined

the bats up for the game, retrieved the bats from the field, packed

everything up going to and from the game, loading and unloading the bus and, back at the school, putting the equipment away for the next time.

It was an exciting end to the season when the Clinton team won the Western Indiana Conference Baseball Championship by defeating Brazil 5-2 in the final game of the year. This game featured a three run rally in the sixth inning to seal the victory. The team won all nine of their games and finished with 6 wins and no defeats in the conference. This outstanding success called for an official black and white team photo by the local photographer. The last day of school the junior high and senior high students gathered in assembly in the gym for awards. For this assembly, the gym floor was covered with a protective cover and metal chairs setup in front of the stage. I sat in a chair located in the middle, towards the back. All of a sudden, I was startled to hear the coach (basketball and baseball coach were the same person) start to tell a story about someone being held in class after school by an English teacher and then having to ride his bicycle all the way to Fairview Park to join the game in progress there. My name was called to come up on the stage with the baseball players and I got a big hand. I wasn't expecting anything (or you can bet I would have sat next to the stage). It turned out that the coach handed me a full varsity Baseball Student Manager letter. Junior high basketball letters were smaller (causing some jealousy among some of my fellow seventh graders). It was the last day of school with really no time to enjoy the moment. My mother sewed the gold "C" outlined in black varsity letter on a gold button-down sweater.

Baseball Student Manager in Seventh Grade

Junior High – Eighth Grade

A traumatic to me event happened in the summer. I had my eyes tested in school and, though I sat in the back of every class, it was determined I could not read the eye chart (well, nothing below the big E). Subsequent trips to the optometrist determined my nearsighted eyes were 20/200 and glasses were in order. (Maybe the reason I missed the basketball shot was I could not see the basket.) Since glasses were a big dollar investment and easily broken, I could only wear glasses when not taking part in activities that might break the glasses, like sports for instance. Unfortunately my eyes were so bad that the lack of eyesight began to affect my baseball. It was said Babe Ruth could read a license plate where others could only make out the color. I don't know how true this was but striking out in baseball became a new norm for me. I now was wearing the dreaded eyeglasses for most everything. I did not think glasses helped my looks at all. I prayed for the day something would be invented so I would not have to wear glasses. The best compliment I remember is one of my classmate girls saying, "Oh, he doesn't look too bad." I was able to translate that highest compliment to "he doesn't look too good." I had at least three plus strikes against me. I was short, with glasses and had severe acne. With my Elmer Blurt sales personality, how was I ever to have a social life? It was very troubling.

I was getting closer to the 16th birthday when I could hit the road.

THE BEARDED LADY

TRIED A JAR

SHE'S NOW

A FAMOUS

MOVIE STAR

BURMA-SHAVE

In eighth grade the Conduct and Effort grades disappeared from the report card. Arithmetic, English/Reading, Spelling, History, Writing, Physical Education and General Science were the subjects. Honorable Mention was again achieved scholastically with A's and B's. I worked extra hard to maintain the "brain" status that I had in math class.

I did run for political office in the eigth grade and was elected secretary-treasurer. What gave me the encouragement to do this I do not know! I had no political gifts and I hated to lose at anything. I don't recall who was the election competition (maybe no one else ran for the office). I do know there was no campaigning, no speeches, etc., or I would have been discouraged from having any part of it. I won the election. Perhaps it was the Smith name. As I recall the class office duties were next to nil.

Basketball Student Manager

Again I really can't remember the sequence of events, but in the eighth grade I became junior high student basketball manager. The good part of this was that I also got to help the high school student manager. He was a high school senior and quite serious about his student manager job. He had additional duties, such as charting where the shots were taken during the game and keeping overall statistics. As a part of the job, I was able to attend all the high school home basketball games as a student manager and also to travel with the high school teams to some of the regular season away games. This turned out to be a basketball season to remember. The dwarf mascot had moved away, so any extra incentive for the team this year had to come from somewhere else.

The season started with home victories over county teams - Cayuga and Dana. Clinton still had trouble beating rival Terre Haute Garfield and lost the first WIC game by a score of 35-44 on their court. Clinton won the next two home games over Otter Creek (Otters) and WIC Linton (Miners). The record was now four wins and only one loss. Then I got to go along on the away game bus trip to Sullivan. The trip was down highway US 41 to the other side of Terre Haute and one of the longest road trips. Sullivan was close to the coach's hometown and he really wanted to win this one. When we got to the Sullivan gym, it was a typical situation at larger schools where the visitors dressed in the girls' locker rooms. Only this time something was very wrong with the sewer system and coming from the shower area was the overpowering, strong, bad odor of sewer. The team dressed quickly and raced out the door to get on the court. The first half went well and the Wildcats took a seven point lead to the locker room at half. Halftime in the odor-filled locker room was abbreviated; the Wildcats returned back to the court quickly with little halftime strategy discussion. During the second half, the game became close. The Sullivan Golden Arrows had narrowed the Clinton lead to two points in the third quarter. Very late in the game with the score tied, Sullivan took the ball down the court and a player fired a shot from way out and at the side of the court. A Clinton player, while trying to block the shot, could not stop his forward momentum and placed his hand squarely on the shooter's forehead. The referee could not believe his eyes at this obvious call. The whistle blew and the signal for two foul shots was given. One of the two ensuing foul shots was made and Sullivan won the game 33-32. Back in the locker room, the coach was in an angry, bad, losing mood. I don't recall exactly what he said, but I do remember he was animated. Completing his short tirade, he then abruptly turned around in the locker room and stormed out the door – but oh - Oh - NO, it was the door into the stinking shower area that he stormed through. In a blur, he reemerged straight out the way he went in.

The school bus drivers would always run the bus to warm it up while the team was dressing. In Indiana, the cool, moist nights caused water to start streaming down the fogged windows. The bus driver's effort was somewhat a waste of time, since the first activity of many of the bus riders was to lower the bus windows so they could see out, lean out and shout outside. Also there were the sneaked "smokes" to be worked in. Smoking was a "no-no" and getting caught would result in being thrown off the team (seemingly an extra challenge to some).

The basketball teams were given a meal after road games. If the trip was short these meals were back in town. If the road trip was long, the meal was where the game was played. I liked the eating out. Our family did not eat out and this was a new experience for me. I especially liked the Italian meals of spaghetti, veal, bread and butter; I could eat my share and then some. After getting back home to the gym and stowing the equipment, I would grab my bicycle from the rack behind the gym and head for home.

The next game was another road trip to Greencastle. Greencastle was a Regional town about the same size as Clinton. This also became a special game to remember. The game was very contested and close. In the fourth quarter near the very end, a lot of player substituting was happening. Our visitors' bench was near the center of the court, next to the scorer's table. Our starting guard was sent back into the game. In the fast and furious action that happened immediately at center court, he grabbed the ball and with a few swift dribbles and deft ball handling, he leaped high into the air and banked the ball into the basket as neat as you please. Only problem – it was the ***wrong basket***. I was impressed that the other guard, a seldom-used substitute, chased after him, grabbed the ball as it fell out of the net, jumped out of bounds, **pointed to the other direction** and fired the ball back to him. But there was not enough time to overcome the wrong-way basket, and Clinton lost the game 47-45. The starting guard was in agony, sobbing, "I'm sorry." It was a sad loss. It was a painful experience. Fortunately, a wrong-way basket is a very, very rare occurrence. I think the box score in the newspaper had an asterisk with an explanation after the basket credit. There was no chance of giving an opposing team member credit for the basket – no one was even close.

Vermillion and Parke County Indiana

The Wabash Valley Tournament had been played since 1916. Rockville won the first three years of the tournament. Clinton hosted the tournament (16 teams) in 1920 and residents opened their homes to house the visiting athletes. Clinton won the Wabash Valley Championship in 1921 beating Freelandville 30-27. No team from Vermillion or Parke Counties had won the tournament since then. The Wabash Valley Tournament was now a large field of 122 teams and small schools were numerous. Small schools had pulled upsets here. Monroe City had won it all last year. The Wabash Valley Prelims were played one week and the Wabash Valley Finals played in Terre Haute the next week. The Clinton coach was becoming well known for getting the Clinton teams up for the tournaments. This was to be no exception. Clinton was always the site for one of the Wabash Valley Prelims. The Clinton Wabash Valley Prelim was made up of the seven Vermillion County teams. (Perrysville in the north part of Vermillion County played in the Attica Sectional of the state tournament). Clinton had won eight straight Prelim's for the Vermillion County Championship before Perrysville won last year. This year the Perrysville Ramblers came in 13-0 and were expected to repeat. By the tournament draw, Clinton played the favored Perrysville in the very first game of the tourney. Clinton proceeded to surprise everyone and won the game by the score of 44-39. Then Clinton easily won over St. Bernice 52-39, and Cayuga 63-45 to win the Prelim and Vermillion County Championship. At the Terre Haute Wabash Valley Finals, Clinton showed good effort and talent by winning over Palestine, Illinois 49-46 and Attica 57-45, before losing to Glenn 33-46 in the semifinal game. Glenn became the Wabash Valley champions by winning the final game 53-24 over Frichton.

Continuing the regular season play, the team experienced a roller coaster run of games, with more games being lost than won. At the very bad end of the spectrum, they lost to Danville, Illinois – Clinton 27 Danville 63. The Brazil game was lost 22-34 after staying close for three quarters. The Brazil game featured the dedication of a new scoreboard in the Brazil gym. The scoreboard showed the names of players and it was reported that it had enough buttons and lights to be a pinball machine. One home game, I was sent to the locker room with a starting player who was feeling sick. Seems he had eaten some bad hamburger before the game. The season ended with another loss to Garfield by the score of 57-46. Flashes of team capability had been displayed but certainly not consistently.

Clinton – 1950 Sweet Sixteen

When tournament time rolls around in March, Indiana is starting to warm up. The windows of the gym would probably have to be opened after the crowd arrived. The old basketball hoops in the backyard become more active with the good outside weather. Basketball excitement is in the air. Seven hundred sixty-six teams have a chance. One game at a time. Just to win the Sectional is everyone's team goal. Clinton, Rockville, Bridgeton, Rosedale, Bloomingdale, Marshall, Tangier, Mecca, Dana, Cayuga, Green Township, Newport, Hillsdale, Montezuma, St. Bernice and Union Township all knew the stakes. Once again the pairing chances fell to the "luck of the draw." Schedules for all the tourneys were drawn by the Board of Control in the presence of representatives of the press. The admission price for the 16 team, seven-session tourney was established at 60 cents for a single session and two dollars and 40 cents for a seven-session ticket. Each team was limited to ten players. Each team was in charge of a faculty manager who was held responsible for their conduct. For a high school with graduating classes of about a dozen, they would have maybe 50 total students in school. With about half the enrollment being boys and with about half the boys still needing a growing spell, you can see how little choice there was in selecting a starting team. Still the tournament was a new start for everybody and every team was going to get a shot at winning a Sectional.

The Clinton Sectional with its 16 teams from Vermillion and Parke counties would require four wins in a row. Clinton and Marshall were touted in the local newspaper as the Sectional favorites. I was once again working to get into all the Sectional games for free and also helping as a student manager when Clinton played. The Sectional games started on Wednesday night with Bloomingdale defeating St. Bernice and Tangier defeating Greene Township. On Thursday night, Mecca defeated Newport and Marshall was upset by Rockville 45-40. At 8:30 a.m., Friday Rosedale defeated Union Township. At 9:45 a.m., Montezuma defeated Bridgeton. At 11:00

a.m., Clinton won in its first round game by a score of 33-24 over Hillsdale. In this game the Hillsdale Hilltoppers tried the slow, stalling game strategy, but it did not work. At 1:00 p.m., Cayuga completed the first round by winning over Dana. Eight teams were now eliminated.

Continuing on Friday at 2:45 p.m., Bloomingdale defeated Tangier to start round 2. Next at 4:00 p.m., Rockville defeated Mecca. The Friday evening session featured the Friday morning victors who would now be playing their second game of the day. At 7:00 p.m., Rosedale defeated Montezuma. At the 8:15 p.m., game Clinton advanced by defeating Cayuga 67-40. It was the third time in the season that Clinton had played and defeated the Cayuga Indians. Twelve teams were now eliminated. Four teams were now in the in the Sectional semifinals.

Saturday afternoon the gym filled to capacity and at the 1:00 p.m., game Rockville moved into the finals by winning a close game over the Bloomingdale Bulldogs by the score of 51-48. At the 2:15 p.m., game Clinton defeated Rosedale 56-38. The Rosedale game was tied 18-18 at halftime. The Cats lead by the score of 32-27 at the third period and turned it on after that. There was a few hour break before the Sectional championship night game. The gym was cleared and the cleanup and sweeping duties were done. I rode home once again on the bicycle for supper and then made the return trip for the finals.

The Saturday night finals game at 8:15 p.m., (the fourth game in two days for Clinton) was close at the beginning. The first quarter ended 12-9 in Clinton's favor. At halftime the game was even closer with Clinton leading 24-22. Following a tied game at 26, Clinton moved out to a 37-29 lead using a balanced scoring attack. Every starter found the range in the fourth quarter and Clinton won 48-37. The game was won with impressive team scoring balance consisting of two players with 11 points and two players with 10 points. The victory was celebrated by the team fans cheering as the stepladder was brought out and the Clinton players and coach cut down the nets. Two Clinton players made the Sectional first team and three others the second team. This was the sixth Sectional win for the coach. It was time once again for the school pep rally celebration and Regional send-off next week.

The state tournament field of 766 teams was now narrowed to just 64. For 702 teams, their seasons were finished. Clinton had the second game draw in the Greencastle Regional. Their opponent from the Attica Sectional was to be tiny Richland Township. The Crawfordsville Sectional winner New Market was to play the Greencastle Sectional winner Greencastle in the other game. Three Clinton players were interviewed by Crawfordsville radio as the excitement started to build for Saturday afternoon. Crawfordsville was the largest town in the Regional area with a population of about 13,000. All-business practice sessions were intense. Pep rallies were held, speeches made and cheerleaders fired up the loyal fans. Clinton fans journeyed to Greencastle for the games to begin.

The little school Richland Township was the people's favorite. We thought odds were against them and their school size was against them. In Indiana the controversy continued as to whether a small school could ever win the state championship again. The talk of changing to school division tournaments by size of the school was becoming more common. Yet much of the Indiana State Basketball Tournament excitement seemed to center around whatever small school was still playing. The Richland Township fans could not and would not miss this game. This could be their year.

The Greencastle team (who you remember defeated Clinton as a result of the wrong-way basket during the regular season) advanced in the first game of the afternoon winning their game easily by the score of 54-45 (28-14 halftime lead).

The Richland Township game was a real battle for the Wildcats. It was trouble all the way. This was a good team. The game was tied 10-10 at the first quarter and Clinton lead by the slimmest of margins 26-25 at halftime. Having raced to a 44-35 lead at the end of the third quarter, Clinton seemed at last to be in control. But the Richland Center players, with great rebounding and shooting, proceeded to even the score at 48-48. Clinton recovered their teamwork and scoring poise and finished ahead with the final score of 60-54. With the ease of Greencastle's first game win and the tough battle that Clinton needed to win, few were giving Clinton a chance in the evening title game. It was felt that this Regional was all but over. It was going to be Greencastle all the way.

The Regional title game started as if Clinton did indeed have little chance. Clinton fell behind and the coach pulled the entire starting five and put in the five reserves. To say the least, this was a very drastic action. At halftime the game looked almost like a carbon copy of the Greencastle rout in the afternoon with the score 28-17. Now even fewer gave Clinton a chance to win. Surprisingly the coach started the five reserves at the start the second half. It did not look good. Had Clinton given up? The first team was returned to the game with the score 30-21. A newly energized first team narrowed the score to Greencastle 39 Clinton 35 by the end of the third period. With four minutes to go in the game the Wildcats completed their catch-up with a lead of 44-43. With one minute and 35 seconds left in the game, Clinton led 49-46. Clinton ran the score up to 55-50 with 30 seconds left. Quick fouls resulted in two more Clinton free throws and Greencastle was unable to take advantage of the their last two possessions. The Regional crown now belonged to Clinton. The regular season wrong-way basket defeat was completely forgotten. A happy team climbed the ladders and cut the nets down to take them back home. It was a real nail-bitter to listen to on the radio. An excited town cheered the results.

Clinton had advanced into the sweet sixteen of the Indiana State Basketball Tournament.

The Vermillion County sheriff met the team at the Lyford "Y" (turnoff to Clinton from US 41) and escorted them over the Wabash River Bridge with the police siren on. A fire truck was provided for the team to ride on. Around 200 fans gathered in the gym for an impromptu, late Saturday night pep rally. This was the third Regional Championship in eight years for the coach. The next step was to play in the nearly 15,000-seat Butler field house in Indianapolis. Clinton was in the Semifinals. They were a member of the sweet sixteen. Their opponent would be the Rushville Lions, who defeated Batesville 47-28 in the Rushville Regional. Rounding out the Indianapolis Semifinals was Indianapolis Tech from the Indianapolis Regional and Madison from the Shelbyville Regional. Since 1946, the Indiana State Finals were also played in the Butler Fieldhouse. This made it even more exciting to play the Semifinals there as part of the tournament leading to the state championship game.

There was further celebration at the beginning of the week as students and teachers from the senior and junior high schools gathered for a speech and yell-filled pep session in the gym. The band was assembled. The pep session was followed by a parade through town. The team rode on a fire truck that was then followed by the high school band and majorettes, cheerleaders, students and teachers in a march from the gym to Main Street and back to the gym (followed by regular classes). To win a Sectional is big and to win a Regional bigger. Clinton and Ellettsville were the only two teams left in the state tournament from the Wabash Valley. A Terre Haute radio station announced they would be broadcasting the Clinton Semifinals game from Indianapolis.

Regional Champs – Sweet Sixteen

Basketball (as in Peach Basket) was invented by Dr. James Nai-
smith in 1891 at the Springfield, Massachusetts YMCA. Basketball
began with 13 simple rules. It spread quickly to other YMCA locations where the leadership and space existed. Indiana basketball
started in the Crawfordsville YMCA in 1893. In Indiana, instead of
climbing up to empty peach baskets, iron hoops were used with
coffee bags for nets. The spread of basketball was hampered by
the lack of places big enough to play the games. The 1907-1908

Clinton basketball team played their first indoor games in a theater building at South Ninth Street and Vine Street. There were widespread complaints about the facilities. For example, it was said the ceiling at Sullivan was so low one of their players could almost reach up and touch it. And it was also said to look out for the four posts. The Clinton team was praised for playing one of their fastest games there and scoring 27 points.

The first Indiana State Tournament was held in 1911. The first championship was won by Crawfordsville. For the first eight years of the tournament the Indiana State Championship was won by teams within 30 miles of Crawfordsville. Clinton is 50 miles away. The games were played inside and outside in a variety of settings. The Indiana High School Athletic Association (IHSAA) was organized. Clinton joined the ISHAA. The first state tournament did not have the approval of the ISHAA. The championship game was played in the Indiana University Assembly Hall with seating for 1,200. The best team from each Congressional District (13) was invited and in the end 12 were represented. Some teams played their way into the tournament. Crawfordsville, the first champion, played Clinton, winning 19-14. At Bloomington, Crawfordsville beat Anderson 36-16,

Walton 31-12, Bluffton 42-16 and Lebanon 24-17. The Crawfordville team record for 1911 was 16 wins and two losses. The ISHAA had at this time 222 member schools. Another noteworthy event in 1911 was the start of the "Greatest Spectacle in Racing", the 500 mile car race in Indianapolis.

In 1912 basketball continued to be big news. Clinton beat Brazil 48-12 to become Fifth District Champions. The team traveled this time to Indianapolis to meet Franklin. Franklin won 16-14 and advanced to the finals. The 1911 runner-up Lebanon won over Franklin for the championship. Clinton had been playing in the Wabash Garage. Their success was creating a demand for a suitable place to play. In 1913 "The Coliseum" was completed for the basketball team. The team did well again this year. The tournament was played on four different playing floors with 77 teams now in the tournament. The winner, Wingate, had an enrollment of 38 and was the first repeat champion. Wingate had no gymnasium of its own. They played two games on Friday and a grueling four games on Saturday to win it all. Clinton played the Wingate in the second game Saturday and gave the repeat champions their closest game while losing

17-13. All of the Wingate points were scored by the Wingate captain with four field goals and nine free throws.

In 1915 the first Sectionals were played with 155 teams entered in the state tournament. By 1920 ISHAA had grown to 621 members and 372 in the state tournament. By 1926 ISHAA had grown to 777 members and 719 were in the state tournament. In 1927 there were 731 entries and for the first time 64 Sectionals and 16 Regionals. In 1936 the 16 team final format was replaced with 16 team Semifinals followed by four team Finals. In 1938 the most high school teams played – 787 total.

This was the third Regional win in eight years for the coach. It would be the seventh trip to the Sweet 16 for Clinton and twice Clinton had reached the Final 8. Clinton lost in 1912 to the Frankfort Hot Dogs at the Indianapolis YMCA.

The newspaper reporters flocked into town for pictures and stories. The coach spent all week explaining his decision to pull the first string players after two minutes of the second period. Clinton had hit only 20% of shots in the first half. But, when the coach handed the game back to the starters, Clinton was only three points worse than when the starters had left. The starters responded by beginning to hit every other shot and winning going away. It was a case of strong medicine explained the coach. The coach said that he was not surprised to win the Regional and that Clinton had not scouted Rushville. He explained the last two times he scouted ahead he had gotten burned. The good Wabash Valley Tournament run was reviewed. The team's teamwork was praised. This team began to feel pretty good about themselves. The Indianapolis newspaper carried stories and pictures.

The overall records of the Clinton Wildcats (19 wins and nine losses) and Rushville Lions (17 wins and nine losses) were not that impressive. The game was expected to be close. Also, everyone knows records didn't really mean anything in a one game elimination state tourney. However, an Indianapolis sportswriter picked Clinton to survive for the night game. Indianapolis Tech (21-3) was favored over Madison (22-2) to also reach the night game. Tech was then favored over Clinton. No Indianapolis team had ever won the State Championship.

The Indianapolis Semifinal games were going to be radio broadcast and televised. The availability of television technology was a major development. After a neighbor showed us his TV and watching TV through the window of a downtown store, it was determined by our family that a TV set was a must-have purchase. Now the world of seeing what went on in Butler Fieldhouse was possible for more and more basketball fans. Whether it would be better than our radio imagination was a question. A family trip to Terre Haute resulted in purchasing an Alden Department Store black and white TV set. It had a square tube, the round tube era being over. A two section iron pole with a large antenna attached was hoisted up the side of the house and attached with brackets and guy wires. The end result in the beginning was faint picture reception from Bloomington and a mostly snowy reception from Indianapolis stations. Imagine this – we were now seeing black and white full-length feature cowboy movies right at home. The Indiana State Basketball Tournament coverage was slowly coming to city, town and farm homes of the masses all over the state of Indiana.

The team practiced hard during the week. It was all serious business as never before. There were close to 1,000 Clinton fans planning to take the trip to Indianapolis. The Cats had the height, speed, drive and talent to win. Go team! Do we dare hope for a win? After all, we had won at Greencastle. The team would be practicing Friday afternoon at the Butler Fieldhouse and housed Friday night at the Indianapolis Athletic Club. This was the big time.

Clinton businesses were urged to close for the team sendoff Friday at 10 a.m. The team, band, cheerleaders, teachers and students gathered with the general public in the gym for the sendoff to the next to last round of the Indiana State Tournament. The school band boomed and the school song rang throughout the gym.

Love and honor to our High School

Our High School old and grand.

Proudly we shall ever hail thee

Over all the land (Rah! Rah! Rah!)

Clinton High School now we praise thee.

Sing joyfully this lay

Love and honor to our High School

Forever and a day!

The Clinton community was energized and loyal. The basketball team was prepared. The team pulled out of town encouraged, excited and hopeful.

The Clinton basketball team took an early lead and held a 17-14 advantage at the end of the first period. But Clinton fell behind for good in the second quarter and trailed at half 29-32. By the end of the third quarter the Lions had extended the lead to 50-42. Three Clinton players fouled out of the game in the last quarter and the team could not narrow the gap. The final score was Rushville Lions 67, Clinton Wildcats 60. On a Saturday in springtime filled with promise, the Cats' dreams were tragically dashed to the ground. Clinton had failed to win in the Saturday afternoon contest. The season was over. No more practice, no more games. No more student manager duties. Back home to something other than tournament basketball for the team, cheerleaders, students, teachers and fans.

Madison defeated the also favored Indianapolis Tech and moved to the final game of the Indianapolis Semifinal. Madison then defeated Rushville to enter the Final Four. Madison, who had three starters back from last year's tournament team that lost in the championship game to Jasper 62-61, once again became the team to beat. This year they did not let it slip away. Madison (26-2) defeated Marion 50-49 in the afternoon game and then easily won the State Championship by the score of 67-44 over Lafayette Jefferson.

A senior and junior high joint assembly was held and the basketball letters were handed out, speeches made and the season wrapped up. I was presented a Junior High Student Manager's letter for handling the Junior High and Varsity "B" Clinton "Kittens" team. It was a great year for me – a lot of experiences and excitement. And I had seen a lot of basketball practice and games. I was very sorry to see it end.

The eighth Grade dance/party was a big disaster to me, just a lot of goofing around. Social life just had to get better. I did not have much time for girls, but that did not mean I wasn't watching and wishing. Girls wore dresses to school, but the dress length was down to a few inches from the shoe tops. Not much to get a look at. Sweaters were a big dress item and they were nice. My mother was the talker in our family. We had many discussions about the lack of social life situation.

As the baseball season started, I again became the student manager of the high school baseball team. This year's team was good, but not quite good enough to repeat at the top of the conference. The team finished second in the Western Indiana Conference. The always present objective of getting out of the last period of school was achieved. The road trips by bus were great.

WITHIN THE VAIL

OF TOIL AND SIN

YOUR HEAD GOES BALD

BUT NOT YOUR CHIN

BURMA-SHAVE

Once again and no surprise this time, I was awarded another varsity Baseball Student Manager's letter. The coach signed my 1950 Clinton Junior and Senior High School Yearbook and wrote a note "Hope you are with us for next four years." With two varsity letters, I suppose I could have bought one of those highly coveted, leather letter jackets. They were very nice black and gold jackets. I don't, however, recall even thinking the thought. Maybe it was too expensive and perhaps I had a lack of interest. Once again the award was right at the end of the school year on the last school day.

There was no formal ceremony for graduation from junior high to senior high. No big deal, I would just be keeping the schoolbooks in a homeroom located in the other building. In many ways I had really enjoyed junior high school.

Completely unnoticed by me was the invention of the credit card in 1950.

Paper Route

Summer again brought some big changes. A neighbor boy mentioned to me that a newspaper route was available. I had been thinking about getting a job and had interviewed at a grocery store. The alarm was set for 3:30 a.m. Sunday morning to go check it out. Jolted out of bed, I was surprised to find just how dark it was at that time in the morning. Quickly dressing, I left the house. I pedaled my way across town on my bicycle, straining to see my way between streetlights in the dark, to an alley downtown between Main Street and Water Street. Water Street was along the Wabash riverbank. There down the alley, in a back room, behind a business, were some wooden benches in a small empty storeroom. The newspaper delivery manager drove up from Terre Haute with a station wagon full of bundled Terre Haute Sunday papers. The paperboy giving up the paper route showed me how to fold the Sunday paper (possible in the summertime when the papers were thinner). We filled the newspaper bag, which had a strap that was wound around a couple of steering knobs attached to the bicycle handles. He also had a pair of "saddlebags" that were designed to straddle the carrier over the back bicycle wheel. These saddlebags would be needed, he said, when the papers are thicker. With only one bag, a trip back for more papers would be required. His sales pitch sold me and I decided to purchase the saddlebags from him. The route started downtown, crisscrossed the center of town sideways, then went west out to Ninth Street, looped back toward downtown, headed south, then looped back again to the west end of town finishing close to my house on Ninth Street. All told, the length of the route was about five miles. The starting point was downtown, about one mile from home and a few blocks from the high school. The pay by the hour was quite good as I could usually complete the route in an hour. Sunday was the best moneymaker, resulting in four cents per paper delivered. On Monday through Saturday I delivered the afternoon Terre Haute Tribune. The paper route qualified as a school work program, allowing me to get out of the last period of school. Friday was the money collection day. Money collection was the worst part of the job because it was required stopping, knocking on each subscriber's door and requesting payment. This made the route take two hours plus on Friday. I had a little green route and collection book for recording customer payments. I carried the book in my back jeans pocket. It was a pain to keep checking it, so I typically would update the book records all at once after getting home. My front jeans pockets would be bulging from the change. I would settle up with the newspaper delivery manager on Saturday afternoon. I kept throwing my profits into my top dresser chest drawer. One day my mother discovered the money and said to my father, "Did you know there is several hundred dollars in your son's top dresser drawer?" My father suggested that I get the money pronto into a Postal Savings System account. We went to the Post Office far more often than the bank. The Post Office offered Postal Savings Accounts and I could go up to the window and make deposits. The account was not a checking account, so I would have to go to the Post Office to get any money out. I was issued a small card with the account number on it and the card had to be presented to withdraw money (no signature or ID was required). I was not used to spending money, so I did not spend any. The account steadily climbed at the rate of about $20-$25 per week. It was great to get home from my paper route on a hot summer day, grab a chunk of cheddar cheese from the refridge, prepare a glass filled with ice cubes and pour a cool Pepsi. We were allowed one eight-ounce Pepsi per day and that's when I had mine. This limitation on soft drinks may have been good practice, as I had never visited a dentist for any reason. I did brush regularly after breakfast and before bedtime. My toothpaste was a box of baking soda that I would dip my wet toothbrush into.

It was the paper route that ended my church attendance. Getting up at 3:30 a.m. and going back to bed at 6:00 a.m. "demanded" I sleep late. I slept too late to go to church, I reasoned. Since my parents had set the early example of dropping me off, they could not say too much. My parents were actually going to church more at this time. Also contributing to my not wanting to go to church were other problems I had with the church. Most of the kids my age had dropped out of Sunday School and there was no regular teacher this year. My previous Sunday School teacher was an older lady, around 80 plus years old, as I recall. Teaching a class of seventh and eighth grade students is a job most younger teachers knew to avoid and did avoid. I did respect and remember her example that she cared enough to try and put those unwilling to shame. The church was an older, large brick building and the sanctuary had pews in the middle and on each side. At the front was the communion rail and raising behind it the preacher's pulpit, and even higher the choir loft. On each side of the choir loft were the pipes of the organ. Above the choir loft was an expensive and beautiful stained glass window with a series of circles as a border and a center circle with Jesus. On one side of the sanctuary were regular opaque windows. On the other side was a very large Tiffany window mural of Jesus walking on the water and seeing this time after time I'm sure had some impact.

And there arose a great storm of wind, and the waves beat into the ship, so that it was now full.

And he was in the hinder part of the ship, asleep on a pillow: and they awake him, and say unto him, Master, carest thou not that we parish?

And he arose, and rebuked the wind, and said unto the sea, Peace, be still. And the wind ceased, and there was a great calm.

And he said unto them. Why are ye so fearful? How is it that ye have no faith?

And they feared exceedingly, and said one to another, What

manner of man is this, that even the wind and the sea obey

him?

St. Mark Chapter 4, Verses 37-41. (KJV)

Tiffany Window – Jesus Walks on Water

The sanctuary also had balcony-seating area at the back. It

was in the balcony that I sat during my junior high years. According

to my mother, I asked to become a member of the church, and I took

the church provided spiritual instruction. I became a member, but I have no recollection of this happening. This surprises me because I have a very good memory of other areas of my early life. Since I showed increasing disinterest in church, my parents encouraged me to consider going to a different church where some of my friends were attending, but I was not interested. I had little spiritual understanding and did not attend church during my high school years.

Senior High - Freshman

I took more interest in the 1951 Clinton football season than usual. The team was much better – winning five, losing four and tying one. My parents were becoming more interested in sports and they started attending football games. My new interest was the after-game action. Out on Ninth Street past the Little Italy area and above a tavern was the Dreamland Dance Hall. There was always a dance after a home game, usually five dances in a year. Although I could not really dance, I did a lot of "looking." There were other boys there in about the same shape. I did have my favorites to look at and sometimes speak to, but after my earlier experiences, I still had no self-confidence and that froze my activities. I wished I had a sister who could teach me to dance. Why didn't school teach us something useful? On the other hand it was probably good it was not taught. I'm not really sure I would have ever become good at it with so little sense of rhythm and no coordination.

Clinton Junior High, Fire Station, Senior High

When high school began, I had to decide what courses to take. My father had gone to college and so I determined I wanted go to college. Therefore my courses were to be college prep in nature. A language was required and I picked Latin over French as the lesser of two evils. My memory was not good and I knew I'd be bored and that Latin would be difficult for me. I was disappointed I could not fit wood shop courses into my schedule. Yes, the Conduct and Effort would be graded for each subject throughout high school. The subject list, oddly enough became shortened to English, Latin, Algebra and History.

There were definitions on the high school report cards for "A" and "F" students as follows:

An "A" Student . . .

Consistently does more than is required.

Is prompt, neat, and thorough in his work.

Takes an active part in class discussion.

Has unusual dependability in taking assignments.

Has initative and originality in working new problems.

Has enthusiasm for and interest in his work.

Has ability to associate and assimilate information.

An "F" Student . . .

Is listless and inattentive in class

Is often tardy with work

Seldom contributes to class discussion.

Fails to do required work.

Often lacks tools and equipment for work.

Fails to grasp general principles of the course.

Is lacking in most of the qualities of the "A" student.

I don't recall any student failures in Clinton High School. I do remember one kid who could not get out of grade school. He was a very strong boy and probably would have been one great football fullback if he could have gotten into high school. He worked for the town trash hauler while I was still in high school.

I was getting excused from the last period of school to go pedal my papers as part of a work program. I could be home usually in good time for supper right after 5:00 p.m. The getting out of bed early on Sundays was not fun for me. I did not want a "graveyard" shift job when I graduated. I still remember the distant, lonely whine of the train whistle as the train rumbled through town about that time in the morning. About the only other noises about town were the numerous dogs barking. Fortunately, dogs were usually kept chained or fenced on early Sunday morning. I learned where the dogs were located after awhile, so I would not jump out of my skin when they fired up barking out of the dark. The worst dogs in my experience were the German Shepards. On one block, there was a quite ferocious (or at least I imagined so) German Shepard that would chase both cars and bicycles. I would get up a good start at the beginning of the block, let fly with the newspaper in the general direction of the front porch and pump the pedals of the bike racing for the next block. The German Shepard would run and bark right at the heel of my foot. I think I was probably in more danger of losing control of the bicycle than of getting bitten. I am not fond of dogs. I think I collected at this particular house every other week and really hoped the people were at home and the dog was inside!

As the basketball season started I knew the coach would have liked me to be the high school student manager. I probably could have lettered all the four years of senior high and gone to every game. Maybe I would have collected many more stories. It had been a very good and exciting experience being a student manager. I had a good example from the last exciting year while helping and watching the previous senior student manager. Being on the bench was really near the center of action. But my dreams of playing were gone and I did not even think at the time of teaching or coaching as possible future career choices. Since I could not play on the basketball team, I had already been student manager, and now was making money at my new job; I decided not to be the student manager. The student manager job was conspicuously posted on the gym bulletin board and I think deliberately aimed at me, but I did not respond. The coach did not approach me about my decision.

I "sold tickets" to the willing and obtained my usual student basketball game pass. The basketball team was without the four senior starters from last year's Sweet Sixteen team. The basketball team's possible success for this year was suspect at best. My parents were now becoming big basketball fans themselves and attended all the games. I would collect for papers on Friday nights and would not get home until after 6:00 p.m. My parents and brother would already be gone by the time I got to the house. In cold weather, I would be typically be frozen. I wore only a light jacket, light socks and light shoes, cotton gloves (if it got too bad) and a pair of earmuffs (if it got even worse). I carried an emergency, fold-up, roll-up, light plastic raincoat should it rain or snow. This was typical Indiana high school garb and to wear more was to be wimpy. I, of course, did not want to be wimpy. Boots would have really been unthinkable. I would come into the house, crank up the thermostat to turn the furnace on and park myself over a large floor register located right over the furnace. My father, the engineer, had rigged a super fan to the coal furnace ducts and the heat would pour out. My feet were ice cold. I would pull off my cold shoes and set them upside down on the register to warm up. Then I would also put my frozen, sock clad feet right on the register. As the heat was applied to my feet they would begin to swell up. When they became toasty and somewhat swollen, I would force them into my stiff, warmed up shoes, grab my coat, turn the thermostat down, jump onto my bicycle and pedal the mile to attend the game. I didn't know what frostbite was. The basketball team started the year by losing five of six games. The loss of those starting seniors was really telling. This was going to be a tough year for the team, cheerleaders, band, teachers, students, fans – everybody.

The paper route now became even more of a challenge as winter really set in. In the winter, the temperature would be typically above freezing during the day and below freezing at night. Riding the two wheel bicycle can become somewhat dangerous. One had to be careful rounding a corner into a shaded area and suddenly hitting a frozen puddle. Turning the bicycle wheel became a "watch out" activity after several spills. Even water puddles became a hazard. Many of the streets consisted of a series of bumpy, previously filled potholes. A little water puddle in the street could hide a deep hole that would provide a sudden, bone jarring bump. The newspaper pickup was moved to a small garage building with swinging double garage doors located downtown by the Wabash River. We were now able to bring our bicycles inside right up to the benches used for folding. The garage had a "pot belly" stove in the center with waist high wooden workbenches on either side. It is a wonder we didn't burn the place down. Whoever arrived first took the responsibility of getting the fire going. Since there were always some old newspapers around, starting a fire was easy enough. Soon the stove was roaring like a train, glowing white-hot until the garage was almost too warm.

What made those early Sunday mornings even worse was that it was totally dark. The Sunday papers got bigger and heavier with advertising as Christmas approached. I would leave the garage with the paper bag on the front handlebars full and each bag on either side of the rear fender stuffed full. It was up hill for the first half block and it took a supreme effort to pedal or push the bicycle up it. Once in awhile a second trip was needed anyway. Fortunately, snow was infrequent. However, any snow was usually a wet snow. Wet snow would tend to accumulate between the bicycle tires and bicycle fenders. If the tires were not kept moving and the temperature was sufficiently below freezing, the wet snow would pack solid between the fender and the tire and eventually would freeze the tire solid to the fender so that it would not turn at all. The bicycle then became a total liability. There was no real way to fix the problem except to get the bicycle into a warm area and thaw it out. Now the bicycle and the load of papers would have to be dragged along. Here again my father helped. If he noticed I was not home around the usual time and the weather was really bad, he hopped into the Little Plymouth and traced the paper route backwards looking for me. Was I happy to see him! When he pulled up, we put the now "useless" bicycle in the trunk, newspapers in the back seat, and I jumped into the front seat where the heater fan was blowing wonderful, warm air at full blast. The heat really felt great and we finished the route with me leaping in and out of the car to toss the papers up to the front porches. Dad was not as available during the week. A paper route is a good life lesson that once you start something it has to be finished whether you want to or not.

If it was a windy Sunday, the thick papers that could not be folded would need to be anchored under either the front porch mats or placed between the screen/storm door and front door. This meant getting on and off the bicycle all the time. Once when I was collecting, a customer complained she did not get the Sunday paper. I reached down and lifted up the mat and there was last Sunday's paper. Sometimes you can do too good a job. After that I made sure some of the paper could be seen. At Christmas most of my customers would give me a tip and these gifts amounted to a total of $100-$125 (I was rich!!!). Most of the money went right to my Postal Savings account for the future.

The Clinton basketball team showed marked improvement by the time the Wabash Valley tournament rolled around. Once again the Black and Gold won the Vermillion County Wabash Valley Prelims – 54-46 over St. Bernice, 48-31 over Newport and 47-46 over Cayuga (who had beaten Clinton 60-51 in the opening game of the season). Clinton had won another Vermillion County Championship. Clinton then went to Terre Haute and defeated Spencer 43-38. However, Ellettsville kept them from reaching the semifinals by a score of 69-53. Ellettsville went on to the final game before losing to repeating champion Glenn.

In a real turnaround from the season start, Clinton's overall record had improved to 13-9 by state tournament time. Expectations were growing. How about another run like last year? Cheer leading pep rallies were held and school enthusiasm encouraged. Clinton proceeded to roll over the little Green Township Aces 64-34 and Tangier Tigers 55-47. This all looked very good. The semifinal game was against the Cayuga Indians again. This time Cayuga turned the rubber game of the season decidedly in their favor 44-36 and the Clinton team had an early exit. The last winner of the 759 teams playing in 1951 was Muncie Central, who defeated Evansville Reitz 60-58. It was Muncie Central's third state title (1928, 1931 and now 1951). Their final record was 26-4. Tournament coverage now consisted of 48 radio stations and three television stations. The Indianapolis station televised the final game of the Indianapolis Sectional, Regional, Semifinal and Final. More Hoosiers than ever before were now able to follow and see Indiana State tournament basketball.

When the baseball season started, I tried out for the high school team. I got someone to cover my paper route and only missed a few practice sessions. However, it became obvious I was not being given much consideration. I felt the coach probably wanted me to be the baseball student manager and was not going to select me as a player. I could have had six varsity student manager letters – imagine a Black and Gold leather jacket with a big block C, the numbers 1954 and six stripes on the sleeve. However, I don't recall that even occurring to me at the time. I used the same decision logic concerning the baseball student manager job as I had for the basketball student manager job, and I went back to my moneymaking paper route. My sports participation was becoming limited to basketball shoot arounds or pickup games in the backyard.

Completely unnoticed by me was the invention of the video tape recorder in 1951.

Senior High - Sophomore

Summer meant going to the drive-in theatre. We did not miss any opportunity to go to the frequent westerns – most of them with Randolph Scott. Some of those nights at the drive-in theatre were pretty warm. At home it was often plenty hot too. We had only the eight-inch oscillating fan. One would sometimes seek a good breeze. An air-conditioned indoor theatre would have probably been better, but they were not the "in" thing (and maybe not that healthy). America was in love with the car. Those pre-World War II cars were really starting to disappear to the junkyards. Newer and more powerful models were appearing. Appearances of the new model cars were big events and we all followed the new car announcements. The drive-in theatre was where you went to show off the new car. For some, the new larger size trunk space was put to sneaky advantage.

During the summer, my paper route kept me busy every day. I followed the Cubs and Cards religiously on the radio. My adventures were limited to my bicycle. However, I did spend some money for a brand new Schwinn bicycle. With shock absorber springs, speedometer and a headlight, it was the finest. Unfortunately, I did have a couple of accidents with it. Going to the little grocery store a couple of blocks away, I hit a rut next to the sidewalk and was thrown sideways into a basement window of a house close to the sidewalk. It was a small window and I did not get into much trouble for breaking it and the bicycle was ok. Then while pedaling the paper route, I crossed a street and looked back to make sure no traffic was coming my way. I then turned forward too late to notice a car backing out of a driveway in front of me. I hit the car rear wheel well. Wham!!! The sudden surprise collision really upset the car driver and passenger, but I was okay. The crash did not hurt the car, but I'm not sure my bicycle front shock absorbers ever worked the same.

My New Bicycle, Less Papers

My Grandparents decided to sell the hobby farm in Marshall and move back to Bridgeton.

Bridgeton, located along the Big Raccoon Creek, was where my father was born. We could travel to Bridgeton by way of what we called the front way or the back way. The front way was to travel to Rockville and proceed to Bridgeton from there. This way provided paved two lane roads all the way and entered Bridgeton over a single lane, 236 foot long, two span wooden covered bridge located over a dam for a large mill. The covered bridge was built in 1868 and was one of 30 plus covered bridges built in the Parke County area from

1856-1920. Parke County has the largest concentration of covered bridges in the world. The Parke County countryside is a scenic drive. The back way was to go through Rosedale and approach Bridgeton from the other end of the main street where the Bridgeton High School was located. This way was partly gravel and at times it seemed as though we were turning right through farm barn lots. The little creeks were crossed using very narrow, sometimes single lane bridges at the bottom of the valleys. Bridgeton had a second street paralleling the main street and my Grandparent's house was on this second street one block from the "business district." The "business district" of Bridgeton is about one short block long with storefronts on each side of the street just before the covered bridge entrance and mill.

The Big Raccoon Creek provided the waterpower for the burr-stone gristmill. The mill has 4 floors. The present mill replaced the mill destroyed by fire in 1869. This mill was not powered by the traditional waterwheel. It was powered by two wooden turbines, each five feet in diameter. The turbines were situated under the first floor where water from the millpond, an area between the mill and the covered bridge, was directed under the mill by the angle of the dam and channeled between the turbines, causing them to counter-rotate as the water moved through their vanes. The water then flowed out the opposite end of the mill and returned to the creek. Turbines were developed in the early 1800's and were considered to be much more efficient than an overshot wheel. The stones were brought into this country in the holds of sailing ships where they were useful as ballast. These stones are a legacy of a bygone era and could not be replaced if destroyed. With proper care, the stones should last several hundred years. The top (revolving) stone weighs 1500 pounds, and the stationary bed stone weighs 850 pounds. The spacing of the two stones controls the texture of the ground grain. It is a simple matter to switch from cracking wheat or corn to making flour.

At one time the mill generated electricity for itself and part of the town. The structure reflects the craftsman of early carpenters. The main beams are hand-hewn hickory and the floor and ceiling joists are yellow poplar.

Bridgeton Covered Bridge and Mill

There were more math classes in College Prep. I was getting good encouragement from my teachers. One math teacher had also taught my father in 1928. I was real sensitive to keeping my reputation as a math whiz. I would study all the problems in the book, whether assigned or not. Often, tests were comprised of un-assigned problems or problems at the end of the chapters. Having already done the problems, I sometimes would be done with the test in just a few minutes and would have to "look busy" for the rest of the period. This was teaching me the advantage of being prepared, with the rewards of good grades. I was not as successful in other subjects. I was not known as a brain and was not as motivated.

This would be my last year of language and no more Latin was something to look forward to in the future. Both in literature and English being an avid reader seemed to be of little advantage for me.

I was not a poet

And I knew it

I did like history, but not having a very good memory kept me from getting good grades. The history often didn't cover much more that the bare facts that we had to memorize. This can be pretty dull stuff. I seldom took books home. I did often study math memory work while gulping down my bowl of flakes in the morning before school. My interest in the basketball pickup games had waned.

Math Class Encouragement

Football was big in 1952. A new football coach had been hired. Tough and athletic he was able to take on the Clinton high school boys without pads. He really showed them how to do it. A good group started to watch practice and follow the team. Late summer practice was held next to the stadium in the baseball outfield. Since practice was close to our house, I watched it often. The first game was away at Linton. My parents knew the new coach through church, so we traveled away to see this first game. Unfortunately the game was won by Linton 13-6. Later this game result turned out to be very important. Linton went on to win the Western Conference Championship. Clinton went on to win all the rest of the their games and finished the season with a nine wins and one loss record. Only one winning game 14-7 was even close. Other games were 38-6, 47-7, 67-6, 40-0, 52-0, 33-6, 31-13, 26-0. It was one great and enjoyable season, but it was a shame to lose that first game. The Dreamland Dance Hall experiences were far from "dreamland like." Now I was competing with upperclassman with cars and those "going steady". I could manage the minimal two-step and that provided a few dance opportunities. These were the days of the "bunny hop" and the "hokey pokey" (was this what it was supposed to be all about?). These might have been invented for kids who could only dance like me, but I was not impressed or interested. Close-up (the closer the better), slow dancing was the only way to go in my book.

Clinton High School Gym and Stadium

Basketball started this year with far fewer expectations. After winning the first three games, the next four were lost. The Wabash Valley Tournament was a disaster. The first game was won over Perrysville by two points. The next game was lost to Hillsdale by one point 52-51. Terre Haute Gerstmeyer won the Wabash Valley Tournament. The 1951-1952 season was finished with seven wins and 12 defeats. With a good "luck of the draw," Clinton won the first two Sectional games 68-44 over the Green Township Aces and 43-40 over Bridgeton Raccoons (I would guess Bridgeton had less than 50 total boys to choose from, and Green Township even less). Then the Wildcats lost to a Rockville Rox team that they had beaten in the regular season by the score of 49-37. No joy over this season. A really large school, Muncie Central, again won the State championship. Small schools just did not have a chance. After beating New Albany 58-57 in the afternoon, Muncie Central easily won 68-49 over Indianapolis Technical in the evening.

Some big changes were occurring as the television pictures began to appear out of the "snow". My father applied his engineering talent to provide a better Rhombic Antenna arrangement. The tin foil that we used to slide up and down the antenna leads trying to boost the signal were no longer needed. TV transmitting towers were taller and had more power giving a wider coverage area. Now we could see Big Ten Indiana University home basketball games telecast by a Bloomington TV station. A Terre Haute potato chip company sponsored the games and "our ticket" was supposed to be a package of potato chips. We were seeing more basketball than we had ever imagined and never missed any of these TV games (and always had our "ticket" package of potato chips with pop). My parents had purchased a new rug for the living room; so we had to watch the games on the living room TV from the dining room when eating or drinking (which was most of the time).

Completely unnoticed by me was the sale of the first diet pop in 1952. I did notice the invention of the hydrogen bomb.

Senior High - Junior

Now class selection improved some. Latin was finished; language study was done, done, done. Chemistry and Physics would be taken the next two years – I would take these in order to **not** take Biology. This year it would be Chemistry. I was able to do especially well in the math aspects of Chemistry and getting good grades in science became a priority. The new classes in Economics and Government did not turn out to be very exciting. I did enter an essay contest in Government and was told it was pretty well done as far as content. But the essay was not submitted because I misspelled too many words. This was the year to get the required two semesters of gym out of the way.

It was at this time I went somewhat sideways with my parents. For years I had read the mail order advertisement offers in magazines like *Popular Mechanics* to order kits for learning how to screen print. This was something I wanted to learn and try. The screen print kit contained all the materials and course instructions. As I recall it was quite expensive with a cost of around $75. I proceeded to order the kit and anxiously awaited its arrival. I'm not sure how I paid for it, but it probably was a money order. The money was no problem; I had been putting money in Postal Savings for quite some time. However, when the package came and my father and mother found out about it, they said it was too much money. My father sent it back and demanded my money back. He was able to get the money back, but that was not what I was interested in. I was not a happy camper. I thought it was my money and there should not have been any problem. I did not always agree with my parents, but I had to admit that I never thought that they did anything that they did not think was in my best interests.

I was able to buy some electronic kits. After the war, a company called Heathkit became very successful manufacturing electronic kits for assembly. I bought and assembled multiband radio kits. I might have been encouraged to do this because my father also had bought some kits. My father had been an amateur radio operator using Morse code while he was in high school. Amateur stations would send an acknowledgement card to other amateurs they had talked to over the short wave stations. He had collected operator's cards from all over the world. He told of the time he stayed up all night to hear if Lindbergh had reached Paris. I also became somewhat interested in stamp collecting. My father had done some collecting when he was in high school and I started with his stamps (which by now were over 20 years old). I got some large mixed stamp packets and sorted and traded some of them. I didn't pursue stamp collecting. I had a better idea as to how to spend my money. What I wanted to do was save up to buy my own car. A car would provide the wheels of freedom.

I was ready to make a big decision. I was missing too many social opportunities by leaving school early before extracurricular activities. I decided I was past the paper route stage of my life. I was well aware "by the hour" jobs probably would not pay as well, but I thought the time had come for change. My brother was ready to take over my paper route.

Stock Boy Plus

I turned the newspaper route over to my brother and applied for work at the largest 5&10 store in town (there were two others). It was the G. C. Murphy chain store and it covered four storefronts on the middle block of Main Street. I started at the bottom rate of 50 cents per hour. The G.C. Murphy pay scale showed that employees could work up to a maximum of 75 cents in who knows how many years. This job was on the punch time clock by the hour. One major, major flaw in my plan was that, once again, my job required I get out of the last class period on the work program.

The G. C. Murphy job title was "stock boy." I found the stock boy title to be more than a little misleading. I would get called when the semi-trucks would pull into the alley behind the store. The alley backdoor lead to a large slide into the basement. The Warehouse

Delivery boxes would be conveyed off the truck to the slide and my

job was to stack the boxes for checking. This call could happen

at anytime, but often was in the evening after the store closed. It

required the bicycle ride one mile to and from the store. I would

"punch in" my card at the time clock when I got there and "punch

out" when finished. After school there would be a row of baskets

loaded in the basement to carry to each counter in the store. Extra

heavy baskets with skids on the bottom – like those filled glass and

crockery dishes or school paper supplies – could be pulled from

the top of the stairs (had to be carried up the stairs) to the various

store counters using a rope tied to the baskets. At store closing the

wooden floor aisles were swept and mopped down with oily brooms.

Once in awhile after hours the wood floors needed to be mopped

and soaked with some kind of oil. Since there was a second floor

storage area over the high ceiling main floor store, there were also

many baskets to be carried up the long staircase to the second floor

for inventory (and back down to the counter when necessary).

Now the job description begins to really get expanded. Upstairs

was a wooden cubbyhole storage rack for glass. The glass was used on the counters to separate the items for sale. The glass pieces were all lengths and conditions. Often it was required to cut the glass to size (sometimes resulting in scrapping when glass was broken or becoming too small a piece to keep). As clerks requested the glass for counter tops, it was hauled to and from the counters. Glass is heavy (and on occasion sharp). Then there were wagons, tricycles, scooters etc. to be assembled for sale. This job was not too bad and could often be done sitting down and at an unsupervised and reduced speed. This type of work often felt more like a break (there were no official breaks except to punch out for meals). Next, there were light fixtures to install in the hardware counter display ceiling, including wiring them to power. Also when there was a sale without inventory, it was required to uninstall a fixture for a waiting customer. This was a good lesson in hot wiring while standing on a ladder. The fish tank required servicing – especially the charcoal filter. Cleaning the filter and the fish tank quickly convinced me fish are a very dirty species. I am not fond of fish tanks. The birdcages were similar problem areas, but the counter clerks took care of the birds and I did not usually have to deal with them. The fire extin-guishers needed to be serviced. They were taken downstairs and the old chemical bottle at the top dumped into the sewer (kinda fun) and a new chemical bottle added at the top (not so much fun). Then the store florescent light fixtures needed new bulbs. Balancing on a 15-foot stepladder was not my idea of fun, especially while trying to look and be cool by not breaking or dropping the long florescent bulbs in full view of everyone.

The candy and cookie storage area was in a screened-off room in the basement. Most of the candies were sealed as they were delivered as bulk candy in boxes to be carried to the candy counter and sold by weight. However, once in a while, some candy or cookies would become unsealed and consequently "available." Of course, one did not want to become caught eating any candy. This was especially true because the store manager was a stern-to-threatening type of personality and firings were known to have happened for far less. One day I saw some inviting and available candy and put some in my pants pocket. I had just started to reach in my pocket and grab a handful of the soft candy when I heard someone coming. I quickly grabbed and thrust a handful, like one does peanuts or popcorn, into my open mouth for a fast refreshment. As I bit down there was a crunch and I immediately surmised something had gone awfully wrong. Ouch. **Ouch.** *Ouch!* I had forgotten that I had been working with carpet tacks and had put some tacks in the pocket before the candy. What to do!! I quickly spit out the whole mess. I was able to empty all the tacks without swallowing any of them. I realized how fortunate that was. I could have been a real headline – "stock boy taken to hospital for removal of tacks from stomach, operation lasted ....circumstances revealed were....." Who says there isn't a merciful God?

In the summer when there were more hours worked, the stock boy's task list was expanded into areas I was even less interested in. For example, I was assigned to the hardware counter to wait on customers. I knew this was probably for two reasons. First, it saved having another clerk during peak business times. Second, the store manager had previously trained stock boys to become assistant managers and probably had this plan in mind. The working as a clerk was one step in the assistant manager training process (as a manager in training I would have been even more of a bargain). With my Elmer Blurt sales technique (they don't want anything, I hope, I hope, I hope), I was very uncomfortable with this job. Also I found that I did not like to be asked questions about something I knew nothing about. Then there was the helping with storefront window displays. While some of this task was fun, like setting up

the candy displays (supplying plenty of opportunity for loose candy),

some display setup was very embarrassing. I'm sure the women

clerks had a good time when I was tasked to setup the female mani-

kins in the window for clothing – especially the women's underwear

displays. I really moved fast when wrapping my hands around the

manikins and putting them in full view window places. I hoped no

one, but no one, I knew would walk past the store "display" window.

If I thought I was going to be seen, I would quickly have to get a

drink of water, run an errand, get lost, anything for a while. I learned

to be very observant of and reactive to the surrounding conditions.

Another high school student in my class was working for a while

with me and this helped make the time more interesting and pass

faster. We would kid with each other and some of the regular full-

time stock workers in the basement with one line "zingers." Good

"comebacks" were developed quickly and we could deliver them

with speech emphasis, straight face and all. I'm sure this became

worthy of an "A+++" if there had been an appropriate high school

course. The problem that developed was leaving these wonderful,

developed talents at work. Delivering a snappy comeback, I have observed and learned firsthand, is in most circumstances considered highly inappropriate. Delivering a snappy comeback with the addition of realism and a straight face can cause some additional problems. Repeated direct quotes from such a performance without the explanation "he was joking" came around to be very embarrassing. When the literal words were repeated back that I had said someone was dumb or stupid (as if it had not been said in jest), it needed to be quickly explained, "I was joking Ha Ha". What about the times it was repeated as literally and no one was not around to give explanation? It was a habit that needed the brakes put on it fast. It did teach me by necessity to try to think twice before saying anything and to be careful about any acting performance (the better the worse) in regular conversation. It also demonstrated to me how difficult it was to break developed habits.

The 1952 Clinton football team was again improved. The defense held the first five opponents scoreless, winning the first four and tying arch rival Garfield 0-0. This team's only loss and another tie were out of the WIC. The team won the Western Indiana Conference title. After game dances became sad old, same old events without improvement.

Driver's License

The junior year was the big one that included the Driver's Training Course. A very worthwhile school course in my mind – teaching something I was really looking forward to using. This was the
event I had been waiting for – the 16-year Indiana driver's license. I
turned 16 the summer before my junior year. The school had a new
Dodge furnished by the local Chrysler dealer. The classes consisted of a gutsy teacher giving lessons to three anxious students.
There were also the tension-filled "private" lessons in the family
"Little Plymouth" with my dad. Parallel parking was a must because
virtually everything in town was parallel parking. I wondered how
people could drive around town relaxed, with their arm out the window (very common in the days of cars without air conditioning). I
learned practice was everything and my confidence gradually grew.

The instructor had a set of brake pedals to over-ride the student, and occasionally needed good reflexes. As I recall his brake pedals were used primarily for teaching students to make a rolling stop become a full stop. We spent many class periods on the two lane roads outside of town.

AT CROSS ROADS

DON'T TRUST TO LUCK

THAT OTHER CAR

JUST MIGHT BE A TRUCK

BURMA-SHAVE

Soon I was on my own with an official Indiana State Driver's License. Since we only had one car, it was not available much of the time. I began, however, to spin around the blocks of the town wasting time, burning gas and listening to the radio. Music on the car radio was great. I especially liked Doris Day's singing.

Work did not interfere with my following Clinton basketball using my usual student pass. Once again the season was so-so with the team winning 10 and losing seven. However, the Wabash Valley Tournament was a good story. Clinton won the Vermillion County title by defeating Dana 49-48, Newport 54-38 and St. Bernice 69-53. Then the team played their way to the semifinals by defeating a couple of WIC teams. First they defeated Brazil 52-40 and then Sullivan 49-42. However, Terre Haute Wiley (another WIC team) beat the Cats in the semifinal 65-46. The Wabash Valley was again won by yet another WIC team Terre Haute Gertsmeyer. Gertsmeyer defeated Wiley 39-37 in the championship game.

Clinton had a respectable record of 15-8 going into the 1953 state tournament. The Wildcats defeated Newport 49-37 for the third time in the season in the first game of the Sectional. However, the Wildcats' season was brought to an abrupt end by the Montezuma Aztecs 51-41. Three straight years without a sectional title. These were hard times. Attica won the Regional and headed to Indianapolis.

Milan – Final Four

The 1953 state tournament did begin to generate some extra excitement. A little school, Milan, was making a run. Milan is located in the southeast part of the state with a town population of about 1,000. They played their home games in another school's gym. Winning their first ever Regional game over Morton Memorial 53-51 in two overtimes, Milan moved into the Saturday night game with Connersville. Playing a "cat and mouse" style of stalling basketball against the high scoring Connersville team, Milan lead by the low, low score of 10-4 at half. Milan scored with five seconds remaining to win the evening game by the score of 24-22. It was the first Regional Championship in Milan history. The next step for Milan was the Indianapolis Semifinal. Milan was right where Clinton had been in 1950.

The Milan team was to play Attica in the second game on Saturday afternoon. Clinton had defeated Attica in the regular season 62-61. In the first game the favored Indianapolis Crispus Attucks was upset by Shelbyville by the close score of 46-44. The Milan vs. Attica game was 29-29 at halftime and even at 45-45 at the game end. Milan then was able to win the game 49-48 in overtime. Wow – little Milan in the Final 8. With Indianapolis Crispus Attucks out of the tournament, who was the favorite? Well, whether the Shelbyville team had a letdown or less talent, Milan amazingly walked away with the Semifinal title with a very one-sided victory 43-21. Shelbyville amazingly hit only two baskets for four points total during the entire game. Milan was in the Final Four. They were for real. Excitement escalated in Indiana as the whole state became aware that a small school had made it to the Final Four. Could Milan go further – they had done so well? Milan's record stood at an impressive won 24, lost 4. By the way where exactly is Milan? It is located down in southern Indiana about 40 miles from Cincinnati. Milan had a 24-year-old coach in his first year at Milan, after two years coaching at French Lick. The new coach brought a new and different basketball style to Milan. He used offensive sets and high percentage shots and it was working.

The Milan Finals competition was big schools. Milan was to play South Bend Central in the first game of the afternoon. Richmond was set to play Terre Haute Gerstmeyer in the second game. South Bend Central's record was 22-5 and their schedule was against much tougher competition than Milan. Richmond had a good record of 24-4 and Terre Haute Gerstmeyer, winners of the Wabash Valley Tournament, were 30-3. Clinton had played Gerstmeyer and lost 48-37 during the regular season as a member of the Western Indiana Conference.

There was plenty of excitement as Milan traveled back to Indianapolis the next Friday. There had been a week of interviews, newspaper, radio and television buildup for the big final games. The TV, radio and newspaper coverage was statewide. The state basketball title of Indiana was within sight. The state of Indiana was set to tune in on the Saturday games. By Saturday night it would be all decided. How did these kids sleep before such important games? I don't know that they did. If so, it was probably because they were high school kids. Milan arrived in Indianapolis on Friday for their workout at the Butler Fieldhouse.

Whether it was the excitement, the competition, an off day or whatever, the Milan game turned out to be a big disappointment. Never really in the game, a disappointed Milan team lost the game 56-37 to South Bend Central. All of us cheering for the small school were very, very disappointed. Maybe it was expecting too much. South Bend Central had reached the championship game for the first time since 1913. Terre Haute Gerstmeyer won the other after-noon game to move to the championship final game. Gerstmeyer gave it all they had in the championship game, but lost the Indiana State Championship by missing a last second shot. South Bend Central won it all by the score 42-41 in a thriller of a game.

On Sunday the realization really started to set in. Much was written about the Milan run. Would this help or hurt the continuing argument as to whether Indiana needed to have class tournaments based on school size. Yes, Milan had shown a small school could get far into the tournament. But, they did not win it all and that was probably too much to ask. But since winning a Sectional was great, a Regional even greater and a Semifinal almost unheard of, there was much to be proud of. All over the state, Indiana boys hit the backyard hoops with a renewed energy. Set shots, jump shots, fast break lay-ups, last second desperation shots, free throws all were practiced over and over. One on one, two on one, three on three, two on three, all sorts of combinations playing pickup basketball. Imaginations had been stimulated and visions renewed. The ball was bounced into the ground with new vigor and shot at the goal with renewed purpose. The small school debate was not over.

When my buddy quit at G.C. Murphy and I saw the stock boy job was getting further into areas I was not comfortable in, I decided I needed to quit. Once again, I reasoned that being available for the last study period and after school activities just might improve my non-existent social life (not much to lose). The problem was how to tell the intimidating store manager that I was quitting and avoid any attempt on his part to try to talk me into continuing. Finally, I decided to tell him on a Saturday night. Saturday night after clos-ing we would lock the store and carry several bags full of money to the bank depository down the block. As we were transporting the money with our hands full and he was locking the store front door, I informed him my last day would be in a week. He stopped and gave me a somewhat stunned look. He asked, "Why?" This was not something I had thought about answering, but this quickly popped into my head, "Too much work for too little money." It turned out

to be a great comeback because he could do nothing about either

one.

Stock Boy Plus Dejavu

I got out of the work program and started to attend the last peri-od of school with wonderful visions of an improved social life. How-ever, one week later I found out that someone from Chicago had bought one of the other 5&10 stores on Main Street. This store was the single front one at the end of the block from G.C. Murphy store I had worked at. It was far less than one-quarter the size of the G. C. Murphy store and was very run down. The new owner was quite ambitious and motivated. He and his brother were trying to start a chain of stores. He had worked for a large chain store in Chicago that had been held up at gunpoint in a daring robbery. That bad ex-perience had been the last straw for him and he decided he needed a change. A small town with a store business and place to raise his kids looked good to him. I saw that this might be an opportunity for me. First of all, I did need to find a way of continuing to make some money. Second, I thought, "I am an experienced stock boy" and where is he going to find one of those in this town? When I met him he quickly jumped at the situation and said enthusiastically to me, "I tell you what, I'll give you a 5-cent per hour raise to 60 cents per hour to come work for me". The next day I was back in the work program and leaving school early. Who knows where my social life would have gone (perhaps there were some leading indicators)? The good news was there was so much stock boy work that needed to be done that I never spent any time in the people-meeting counter and cash register work. The owner and I worked past 11:00 p.m. many nights getting the store in shape. The hours mounted up. Then there was Saturday from 9 a.m. to 9 p.m. No one worked on Sunday. Now I was making money and had no time to spend it. This time-consuming job probably also kept me out of all kinds of trouble. However, my social life stayed at nearly zero.

This stock boy job was expanded in some ways also. There was carpentry work, shelf assembly, price marking, cleanup, setup, fix-up, display design, and you name it. This store also had a storage area above the store up a flight and a half of stairs. Even for a growing boy the work was a challenge at times after long hours. Much of the time I was just given general instructions and left on my own. Instead of semi-truck delivery, the owner would drive to a warehouse distributor and bring back loads of merchandise. Freight shipments would arrive for checkout and stocking. When the owner bought the store, there were some "mystery" items on the shelves and he had no idea what they were. The collection of enameled pot commodes was puzzling to him. He was assured there was a need. Then there were farm items such as handgrip corn shuckers, less of a need for these types of items for sure. There were items that had been in the unsold stock for years. The store inventory was pretty much a start-over proposition. My job working with this owner was almost too much of a joy. He seemed to have unlimited energy and enthusiasm.

I was able to use the Little Plymouth for spins or once in awhile to go to work. Mostly it was just driving around doing nothing. Once while wheeling for driving sake out of town and circling back late at night with a couple of my buddies, a large dog suddenly flashed in front of the car. I hit the brakes but the dog hit the front of the car dead center. The dog rolled over the bumper and caved in the front fender. I stopped the car and going back we found the dog dead at the side of the road. There was no way of knowing where he came from. There were no lights nearby. Heading back after inspecting the car and finding the damage, I remarked, "I hope it was not a valuable dog." One of my buddies answered, "It was probably a mongrel." "Oh," I said, "Are they very valuable?" My buddies thought that was very funny, I did not know what a mongrel was.

SLEEP IN A CHAIR

NOTHING TO LOSE

BUT A NAP

AT THE WHEEL

IS A PERMANENT SNOOZE

BURMA-SHAVE

Having saved my money, I had more than enough to buy a car and insurance. I became frustrated with my father's procrastination about my getting my own car and threatened to just go and do it on my own unless he cooperated. Dad went to the local car dealer and tried to find a "good deal." With my Elmer Blurt personality, I certainly was not up to dealing with a car dealer to buy a used car. What my father picked out was not something I would have selected. His version of a "good deal" was a reasonably priced used car with low mileage and not likely to need maintenance. This turned out to be a 1942 Plymouth Sedan with an aluminum sun visor mounted over the windshield. It was manufactured at the very tail end of car production before all car production was converted to making military equipment for World War II. The car had been owned by an older couple and had low mileage. It had been polished to the point where the paint was worn thin. It was a faded, pale blue color. I paid about $800 for it, as I recall, and with another $500 plus for a year's worth of insurance, I was at last on the road with my own car. Never mind what the car was like, I was not going to complain. Trying to jazz the car up, I gave it a two-tone paint job using a brush. The main body was maroon and the top a light gray. I assure you that there were no other cars like it out there. The car didn't look too bad at a distance. Now I could retire the bicycle. I also didn't need

to borrow the family car. And I still had plenty of money in Postal

Savings. My senior year was looking up.

My 1942 Plymouth Before Painting

My 1942 Plymouth After Painting

IF A TRIP

TO MARS YOU EARN

REMEMBER THERE IS

NO RETURN

BURMA-SHAVE

In the spring it was mushroom hunting time. Ever since we were small kids, my brother and I had gone mushroom hunting with our parents. We looked for "woods" mushrooms that were typically with a long stem and sponge-like top. We looked for morel mushrooms that looked like little sponge trees and came in various sizes. The cap has distinctive ridges and pits, resembling a honeycomb or pinecone and the entire mushroom is hollow. The color can vary from tan to a honey gold. The morels camouflage themselves well and this adds to the challenge of finding them. Over the years we had favorite places to look that in past years had yielded results. Knowing where to look also helped to discover the time to

look each year. There was nothing to eat as good as mushrooms.
After picking them, mom would cut them in half and soak them in
salt water to get any bugs out of them. Then they would be covered
with egg whites, or egg whites and yokes, and Ritz cracker crumbs.
Then the mushrooms would be fried. Mmm good! It seemed we
could never find enough of them. A small batch would be fried with
scrambled eggs.

Springtime with all those romantic songs on the radio was hard
to take. I noticed my younger brother was not having the social
problems that I was experiencing. My brother also did not have the
musical problems, as he was now a member of the Clinton High
School Band (our father had also been a member of the Clinton
High School Band).

My Brother the Musician

Completely unnoticed by me was the invention of radial tires in 1953. I did notice the invention of the transistor radio.

Senior High – Senior

The senior year started with the reassuring knowledge it would be the last year of high school. I was ready to move on. The stock boy job continued and I never saw a last period the whole year. Since I was continuing with the College Prep program, I had few optional classes to choose. I had successfully avoided Biology. I took a class in typing. I thought that typing would be useful and always come in handy. However, typing somewhat proved my lack of mechanical dexterity and was frustrating. I still contend I had a malfunctioning mechanical typewriter that threw in extra spaces.

With a new football coach (success having resulted in a better job at our arch rival Garfield for the previous coach), the football team started off okay with four straight wins, including two against

Terre Haute teams, but then finished 5-4-1. The dances after the home games proved to be better than usual. I now had a car of my own to get me to and from. I even found some girls to ask for a slow dance on a somewhat of a regular basis. But still not much going as far as a real social life.

Many aimless driving trips were taken up and down Main Street and out into the countryside. Once we decided to go to Paris (just across the border in Illinois). While circling around the streets of Paris, one of my buddies leaned out the window and yelled at some girls walking down the street. The next thing I knew there was a red light flashing in my back window. Pulling over to the side, I rolled down the window for the policeman. He asked, "What is with that yelling at girls, what if one of them was your sister or daughter?" I don't think we related too well with his line of thinking. He stated, "I think you better turn this car around and get back to Indiana." After stating, "Yes, sir," I rolled the window back up, put the car in gear and turned at the next corner. One of my buddies, who knew more about Paris than I did, quickly informed me that this is not the fastest way out of town. That probably explained why the police car turned and was still visible in the window following right behind me! I said,

"It may not be the fastest, but I going back the only way I know, the way I came in." I was very careful not to speed (the few minute trip at 15 to 25 miles an hour was a very anxious experience and seemed to take forever). The police car turned back when I cleared the city limits. My buddies liked to refer to this night as the night we were thrown out of the state of Illinois.

DINAH DOESN'T

TREAT HIM RIGHT

BUT IF HE'D SHAVE

DYNA-MITE

BURMA-SHAVE

I began to really look forward to going to college. Although nothing formal was setup, I thought I would be going to Purdue, where as you recall my father went. I had no idea what I wanted to do, only plenty of ideas, fully developed, as to what I did not want to do. Engineering seemed to fit with my college preparatory courses and my good grades in math. My overall class standing and grade level was in good shape for entrance. Purdue is an Indiana State Land Grant School with a very reasonable in-state tuition cost. I could take all the credits I wanted a semester for $90 (and this fee included tickets to Big Ten sporting events football and basketball and intramural fees). The other possibility considered was Rose Poly Technical in Terre Haute. My math teacher was pushing the Terre Haute alternative and arranged for me to attend the senior day tour. Rose Poly had a fine engineering reputation and I could live at home. That last part was a real turnoff for me. I wanted to get away. There was no social life in sight staying home and I had had enough of nothing. Somehow I had to break out of this zero social life situation. Seventy-five miles away in a large coed school would be just fine. I could hardly wait. Visions of (never mind) danced through my head. This was reinforced when a schoolmate, know-ing my interest in Purdue, invited me to go with him and his father and his father's friend to a football game. Purdue played Michigan State (the football powerhouse that year). We got there early and while the adults did their thing (in the only bar close to the campus, I think), the two of us explored the campus. It was a great day and reinforced my interest and imagination of going to school there. The football game was close and exciting. At one point in the game and right in front of us, a Michigan State player raced around end toward the goal line as a Purdue player circled out of the end zone to meet him. It was the hardest collision I had ever seen in a football game. Both players were down. This was real hardnosed football. Purdue could not quite pull off the win, but did quite well considering their apparent smaller size. Indiana has some great fall weather and it was one fine time.

In November, my grandmother in Cloverdale became ill and after a difficult two weeks she passed away at the age of 88. The funeral was on cloudy, cold winter day in Cloverdale and she was buried in Spencer. There were eight grandchildren and 13 great-grandchildren. This was a sad time for the family. It was my first experience of losing a family member.

The 1953-1954 Clinton basketball season did not look very promising. Three years without a Sectional title had really dampened expectations. Maybe this was the year for the Wabash Valley Tournament. Entering the Wabash Valley Tournament with an even record, Clinton proceeded to win the County Tournament again by defeating Hillsdale 59-44, Newport 61-52 and Dana 54-50. However, in the first game in Terre Haute, Clinton was defeated in a close game by Chrisman, Illinois 48-47. The Valley Tournament Champion was the basketball powerhouse Terre Haute Gerstmeyer, who won the championship for an impressive third straight year.

This was the first year I needed to file a Federal Tax return. In 1953 I had earned a total of $1002 from G.C. Murphy and Horney Variety Store. I had to pay $69 in Federal Income Tax, becoming a tax-paying United States citizen.

Late in the regular basketball season, Terre Haute Gerstmeyer came to the Clinton gym for a WIC game with the Number One ranking in the state and an undefeated record of 22-0. What developed was completely unexpected. As I recall one of the Gerstsmeyer (or Tech as we more often referred to them) players was out sick. Still it had to be called a huge upset when Clinton won the game 37-35. We could hardly believe our eyes. Several horn-tooting celebration drives up and down Main Street were in order. Clinton was on the Indiana basketball map – this victory had to be noticed by everyone in the state. Terre Haute traveled out of state the next week and lost another game. Clinton finished the season with an overall record of 12 wins and nine losses. It was time again for the state tournament. Clinton started the tournament by winning close games with Cayuga 54-51 and Rosedale 45-40 to reach the semifinals of the Sectional. This was the last chance to see my school win a Sectional during my high school career. How could they lose four straight? It seems they had it all figured out and Clinton lost the Saturday afternoon game to the Mecca Arabs by the score of 51-43. That evening Montezuma defeated Mecca for the Clinton Sectional title and it was the Montezuma Aztecs celebrating by climbing the ladders and cutting down the nets.

I now felt pretty good about my freshman decision to drop the student manager activity – or maybe I could have made a difference (I doubt it). The largest school in the Sectional and my hometown high school had failed for all four years of my attendance. Clinton had not only failed to win the Sectional, they had not even managed to reach the final game of the Sectional. Small schools certainly weren't doing so badly in this part of the state.

Milan – Again

Muncie Central with a record of 15-5 was favored to win the state. They had the track record to pull it off. They had played one of the toughest schedules in the state. Muncie Central was the recent Indiana State Championship winner in 1951 and 1952 and they were confident this championship was theirs for the taking. Reading the sports pages revealed that little Milan had repeated as Sectional champions. Milan's Regional game was at Rushville and they were to play Rushville in the first game.

The Montezuma Aztecs proceeded to defeat two other small schools in the Greencastle Regional, winning 55-52 over Filmore and 70-61 over New Ross. The Regional champ Montezuma was going to the Indianapolis Semifinals.

Across the state and even more astounding, the news came that Milan had repeated as Regional champions. Easily beating Rushville 58-34 in the afternoon, Milan then defeated Aurora using a fourth quarter scoring spurt to win going away by the score of 46-38. Milan scored an incredible 18 points to Aurora's four points in the fourth quarter. Aurora had previously handed Milan one of their two defeats in the regular season by a score of 54-45.

This all set up the Indianapolis Semifinal with Montezuma Aztecs (23-5) vs. Milan Indians (24-2). It was a rare Sweet Sixteen small school vs. small school game. A small school was now assured of getting into the Final Eight. In fact, in this match up, Milan was the big school. Montezuma had just 36 boys in high school and Milan had 76. Milan was twice as big. Some said that one player on the Montezuma team could have been mistaken for a team mascot. As the smallest school, Montezuma became a crowd favorite. Montezuma was the first Parke County School to reach the Semifinals in Indianapolis.

The sportswriters and media were thrilled. The fans were thrilled. TV coverage was continuing to grow even bigger – more people were going to witness these games than ever before. There was one other big fact to be considered – the Milan team had been there before. Milan and Terre Haute Gertsmeyer were the only teams left in the tournament from the 1953 Final Four. South Bend Central, the 1953 Champions, and Richmond were out of the 1954 tournament of 751 teams.

The Milan Indians lead the Montezuma Aztecs at halftime 29-21. With the lead, Milan went into their "cat and mouse game." However, it was backfiring as Montezuma, before 14,000 plus screaming fans, pulled to 32-30 at the end of the third quarter. As the game progressed Montezuma was forced to foul and Milan was more than ready to put foul shots through the net. Milan won the game by the final score of 44-34. Montezuma had duplicated Clinton's success in 1950 and like Clinton had failed to win the afternoon game. Playing in the first Saturday afternoon game this year, Milan could now await the winner of the second game. Crispus Attucks (23-4), who lost in the afternoon game last year, was playing Columbus (21-5) this time. Milan had beaten Columbus during the season 52-49. Milan must have been thinking Columbus would be a good opponent in the finals. However, this year Crispus Attucks came back from 14 points behind to win with a free throw by the score of 68-67. It was Crispus Attucks that Milan would be playing in a couple of hours.

The Crispus Attucks team was an unknown to Milan. Milan would have to be up for this one. Crispus Attucks had rolled over a lot of teams. Milan trailed 17-16 at the first quarter, but managed to be ahead 39-32 at half. Milan could play a fast paced game if need be and if the percentage shots they were disciplined to take were there. But, from a strategy viewpoint, it was often the Milan "cat and mouse game" that frustrated teams. It especially frustrated opponents that liked to play fast. A few disciplined and often easy baskets without a response late in the game and a must foul situation would begin. Milan played the "cat and mouse" well and went on to defeat Crispus Attucks 65-52. Milan was into the Final Four for the second straight year! Once again, however unlikely, they were Indianapolis Semifinal Champions. However, Milan having been here the year before was careful to temper their celebration. The Milan team had their sights set higher this time. Could they do it? Most thought, "I doubt it." Most said, "I hope it."

Who else was there in the Final Four? Well there was Terre Haute Gerstmeyer back again, runner-up to South Bend Central last year, they also had set their sights higher. A Terre Haute school had never won the State Championship. Gertsmeyer had a re-markable 31-2 record. They had played teams all over the state and even had played two games outside the state. Oddly enough only Clinton had defeated them in state. Lexington, Kentucky from out of state also had defeated them. To travel that extensively in high school was very unusual, but Gertsmeyer had been having good years and sought out competition. Gertsmeyer had won three straight Wabash Valley Tournament Championships. Their closest tournament game this year was in the Sectional where they de-feated Terre Haute rival Garfield 44-42. Garfield, Clinton's biggest rival, defeated Clinton 75-53 during the season. Gerstmeyer Tech was also on a mission. It was Gerstmeyer that Milan would play in the second afternoon game. In the other game Elkhart (25-3), who had knocked out defending champion South Bend Central, was to play Muncie Central. Muncie Central had defeated Elkhart 59-53 during the season. It certainly looked like Muncie Central was on track to take it all.

If you think the build-up before now was big, the hype was now at a fever pitch. One week and the results will be in. Who will be the Indiana State basketball Champion? How would these high school kids respond? What does it take to get ready for Saturday? How does one stay calm? I sure didn't know. My no rim, no net, no rim experience was certainly of no help. I couldn't imagine. I could only hope. If it could happen it would certainly be the biggest sports story I would ever know about. Milan was the people's favorite again.

Saturday, as usual, I went to work. I worked Saturday afternoon, eagerly both fearing and awaiting the results. At last someone knew the scores. The first game was won by Muncie Central 59-50. Muncie Central was in the Finals for the third time in four years. Then the word came of the second game. Milan had won!!! They had pretty much lead all the way, winning 60-48. Terre Haute would continue waiting for a State Championship. That set the stage for the BIG Game. Again, this was for all the marbles, as they say. The Indiana State Championship – the last team standing out of a field of 751 teams at the start of the tournament. A chance for real history in the record books. A chance for a small school to do the impossible. I went to the storeowner and asked to get off early. As I recall he was quite agreeable. I think I would have considered quitting if he hadn't of been agreeable. After all I had already missed two games that day. I headed home for the TV. I wasn't going to miss this game but honestly my gut feeling was that I would be disappointed. Would it be like last year? Would it be like Christmas, where much of the excitement is the anticipation?

How were the players reacting? How could one eat a meal getting ready? Maybe it was good they had to get right back out on the court a few hours after the afternoon game. There was not much time to think about it. A very excited group of 14,000 plus, lucky-to-be-there fans walked back into Butler Fieldhouse. An even larger excited group of fans gathered around their TV sets, thankful for the technology that gave them the opportunity to see this game. Many would still rely on gathering around the radio to get the play-by-play results. How was this game going to go? What was about to happen? Favorites really meant nothing. Records meant nothing. Anything could happen. Bring it on!!! The Indians and the Bearcats. The Bearcats and the Indians. David and Goliath.

Milan struggled to a 23-17 halftime lead. They were helped by the Muncie Central shot selection resulting in a poor shooting percentage. So far, so good. All in all it was not a bad position for the Indians. Only one half to go. They can do it! What do you say and do at a halftime of such an important game? Remember the Milan coach was only 26 years old with four total years of coaching experience. Whatever he had been saying and doing was certainly right. We thought last year was big, but look at this year. We were inching toward the climax. All Indiana was watching and waiting. Time to get whatever was needed for the second half. I was already full of potato chips and drank my one coke allotment. It was hard to sit still. Time for the second half.

Milan didn't go full "cat and mouse," but they did become more deliberate. Muncie Central was a good team with good players. The Muncie Central team was more settled in the second half and gradually got back into the game. At the end of the third quarter the score was tied at 26-26. Oh-oh. The game was slipping away from the Milan Indians. Muncie Central went ahead 28-26 on free throws. IT WAS SLIPPING AWAY!!! Then the Milan coach ordered the team to stall. Milan stood still with the ball. Hey, this is no time for "cat and mouse," you are BEHIND. Over six minutes remained. Muncie Central did not go after the ball. They reasoned we are AHEAD. The players stood and looked at each other. The fans sat in shock. I leaned forward at the TV, I needed to move closer. What was going on? Well, I thought, they will never put this in a movie - it wouldn't look real. Minutes pass equally on the game clock and on our wall clock. With about three minutes to go, Milan resumed play. At about two minutes, Milan tied the game 28-28. Then getting the ball back and hitting two free throws, Milan now went into the lead 30-28. About one and half minutes left. Milan again gets the ball back and it looks like they will seal the game with a lay-up, but the ball rolls off the rim. Muncie Central grabs the ball and a few seconds later ties the game at 30. Now there are 48 seconds left. Was this one not to be? Why didn't that lay-up go in?

Timeout was called. The Milan team huddled around their young coach and set up their last play. Muncie Central had to be careful and not foul. They know Milan wins games with foul shots. The game resumes. The clock ticks down, down to the last few seconds heading to 0. A fake, a dribble, a jump shot (just like a thousand times in the backyard) and the basketball is in the air, reaches the top of its arc, starts falling toward the basket and - no rim, just bottom of the net - Milan leads the game 32-30. No Muncie Central time-out, just shock, and then the game-ending buzzer. Milan had won! They HAD WON! It was unbelievable, the impossible, the Milan miracle. The scene at Butler Fieldhouse was bedlam. The scene in many homes was the same; I was not able to sit. All over Indiana fans were not able to sit. This was history, what a story, and I knew I would never forget this. This would be forever the greatest sports story I would ever witness. The Milan team remained on the court for a long time, mobbed by the media and excited fans. There was the medal ceremony and the presentation of the Indiana State Championship Trophy and the climbing of the ladder for the cutting down of the nets. It was all over and what an ending. This surely should silence those who advocated dividing the tournament according to school class size. Little Milan had shown it could be done. This is the smallest school to win since 1915 Thorntown. What an example of dreaming about and getting the impossible.

The next day Milan headed back home, a two-hour trip home on two lane roads. They were greeted all along the way by enthusiastic basketball fans. The roads to Milan were jammed with cars and cars were parked along side of the road. There were people everywhere. Thousands of people, maybe 50 to 100 times the population of Milan. A stage on a truck and a microphone was all that was needed for the homecoming celebration. The coach and the players, young high school teenage heroes, were center stage and took their turn at the microphone. I'm not sure many fans had any voice left. However, as is often the case, the speech long to be remembered was an unplanned single sentence looking toward the future. The coach's wife simply spoke wisdom into the microphone, "It's nice to be important, but it's more important to be nice." Here was something else to remember on a great day, celebrating a great achievement.

Shooting basketballs in the backyard continued for me. Seeing what was now being called "the Milan Miracle," winning of the Indiana State championship on TV, had been a great experience. As spring warmed up Indiana, I now looked forward to graduation.

Completely unnoticed by me were the invention of oral contraceptives and the opening of the first McDonalds in 1954.

Bread was now 17 cents per loaf, gas 21 cents per gallon, stamps were 3 cents and the average yearly wage was up to almost $4,000. I was tortured by the music of the times: *Secret Love* (Doris Day), *If I Give My Heart to You* (Doris Day), *Teach Me Tonight* (Jo Stafford), *I Need You Now* (Eddie Fisher), *Make Love To Me* (Jo Stafford), *Hold My Hand* (Don Cornell), *Stranger In Paradise* (Tony Bennett), *Mr. Sandman* (The Chordettes), *Little Things Mean a Lot* (Kitty Kallen), *Three Coins In A Fountain* (Four Aces), *Young At Heart* (Bing Crosby), *If You Love Me – Really Love Me* (Kay Starr), *The High And Mighty* (Les Baxter), *I Get So lonely - When I Dream About You* (The Four Knights), *Hey There* (Rosemary Clooney). It is a wonder I did not go crazy!

I was accepted to enter Purdue in the fall. Our family visited the campus for High School Day tour and I was impressed with the various school demonstrations. I was leaning toward Civil Engineering because I had read more books about Civil Engineering Projects, such as the Holland Tunnel, Brooklyn Bridge, Golden Gate Bridge, etc. It was a big school and that was what I wanted. We toured the Electrical Engineering building where most of my father's classes had been held. Coming from a small town I had no idea what to expect and, therefore, I suppose I had no fear. My mother always said I was not lacking for big ideas.

I did go to the Junior-Senior Prom. It was mainly to be able to say I had been to the Junior-Senior Prom. I had not gone as a junior and did not want to miss the event. We double-dated and I didn't drive. My date was a nice looking, popular junior girl. However, I did not feel she really wanted to be with me and that pretty much turned me off. She was one of the girls I had asked for some of those slow dances back in Dreamland Hall. Nobody took any pictures. When it was over, I was able to say I had been to the Junior-Senior Prom.

Keeping the car shined was an ongoing task. I learned to change the spark plugs and points, oil and oil filter, and at several inconvenient times, the tires. It was good to have my own car to get to and from work and cruise in between.

USE OUR CREAM

AND WE BETCHA

GIRLS WON'T WAIT

THEY'LL COME

AND GETCHA

BURMA-SHAVE

There was the senior picnic at Turkey Run, an Indiana State Park in Parke County a few miles from Marshall. It is a popular park with trails and a suspension bridge over Sugar Creek. This was a fitting last social disaster of high school. A baccalaureate service was held. The graduation ceremony for 106 seniors was held in the gymnasium. The boys were in royal blue gown and the girls in white. We marched in procession led by the faculty and high school band. The ceremony started with an invocation. Among the skits put on by the seniors was one about God's House and included the reading of the 23 Psalm. The high school choir sang *You'll Never Walk Alone* to send us into the world with hope in our hearts. Numerous awards were announced, the diplomas were given and a benediction closed the time together. High school was all over but the shouting.

Graduation – Free at Last

A trip was needed to West Lafayette to find a place to stay. My father had lived in private housing when he attended Purdue and that looked like the best route for me also. Another Clinton senior classmate was to become my roommate. He also was going into engineering. There were entrance exams in English and Mathematics. I rated average in English. However, using some of my "a little preparation ahead" technique I scored in the upper math range and was given five credits before starting. My first math class was to be Analytical Geometry.

I spent the summer of 1954 in the 5&10 variety store working and saving more money for college. I could not wait to start. I thought this would be a new beginning for me. Meeting and being with the right girl was very important to me. Part of my problem I'm sure was that I was too serious about it. Surely my social life would pick up for me at college. A college education would also be nice. I had never spent a night away from home without my family.

Looking Back

I didn't regret my decision to not have six varsity letter years as student manager. I didn't regret my decision to get out of the newspaper business. I didn't regret my turning down retail opportunities. And I didn't regret graduating from high school. I tried not to regret my lack of social life. In short, I was ready to move on. Where this Indiana raised boy ended-up is for another story.

I have recovered (at least that is my belief) from my illustrious basketball career consisting of one disastrous shot. Maybe competition was what it was all about. It is for me to imagine what those Indiana basketball heroes experienced to have family, friends, classmates, cheerleaders, teachers, community fans for all kinds of reasons, even stranger bystanders, cheering and shouting encouragement. I have heard that when a believer gets to heaven all the angels rejoice and maybe even sing. I'm not much for singing, but what a sight that will be. Being later concerned about sin and pleasing my Creator (a righteous, loving God, plainly revealed in His Holy Scripture), I found no one comes close to obeying God's laws – nobody hits rim or net. Jesus said, "I am the way, the truth and the light" and He (alone) will slam duck you to Heaven by grace (only if you trust Him). God is for me (another bit of the impossible). Using my father's example (when he rescued me on my paper route), Jesus will pull-up someday (in something better than a Little Plymouth) and stretch out His hand. He will throw my useless baggage in the trunk and we will ride off with the victory already won by Him into a new eternal world, another new start full of His promises. Will there be basketball there? I don't really know. I do know He knows all about it. If not, imagine this if you can, there will be something better!

I left Indiana when I graduated from college. I have looked back; it is a part of me. Only in Indiana is it probably a sin not to touch rim or net. **Basketball: King of Indiana**.

ABOUT THE AUTHOR

Gary graduated from Clinton High School, Clinton, Indiana in 1954, Purdue University, Bachelor of Science Electrical Engineering in 1958 and St. Louis University, Master Business Administration in 1966. He was married in 1959 to Freya Lieurance. They have four children – Bobbie, Judy, Ross, Matthew, and eight grandchildren. His engineering career spanned 1959-1966 with McDonnell Aircraft. His computer management/consulting career spanned 1967-2000 with Control Data, Compucare, Northwest Aerospace Training Corporation, Northwest Airlines, Jostens, Keane and others. Gary was president of his own corporation. Gary has resided along the way in Indiana, Missouri, California, Virginia and Minnesota. He is currently retired in Minnesota and the autobiography about growing up in Indiana basketball country is his first book.

Printed in the United States
53194LVS00007B/46